Life, Law
and Letters

Also by
Louis Auchincloss

Fiction

The Indifferent Children
The Injustice Collectors
Sybil
A Law for the Lion
The Romantic Egoists
The Great World and Timothy Colt
Venus in Sparta
Pursuit of the Prodigal
The House of Five Talents
Portrait in Brownstone
Powers of Attorney
The Rector of Justin
The Embezzler
Tales of Manhattan
A World of Profit
Second Chance
I Come as a Thief
The Partners
The Winthrop Covenant
The Dark Lady
The Country Cousin

Nonfiction

Reflections of a Jacobite
Pioneers and Caretakers
Motiveless Malignity
Edith Wharton
Richelieu
A Writer's Capital
Reading Henry James

Life, Law and Letters

Essays and Sketches

Louis Auchincloss

Houghton Mifflin Company
BOSTON 1979

Library of Congress Cataloging in Publication Data
Auchincloss, Louis.
  Life, law and letters.

  I. Title.
  PS3501.U25L5   809   79–14642
  ISBN 0–395–28151–2

Printed in the United States of America

Q 10 9 8 7 6 5 4 3 2 1

The author is grateful for permission to reprint as follows: "Origin of
a Hero" was first published under the title "Writing the Rector of
Justin" in *Afterwords,* Thomas McCormack, ed., copyright © 1969
Harper & Row, Publishers, Inc. "Jane Austen and the Good Life" was
first published as an introduction to *Persuasion,* copyright © 1977 by
The Limited Editions Club, Westport, Connecticut. "Dreiser's Love of
America" was first published as an introduction to *Sister Carrie,* copyright © 1969 by Bell & Howell Co., and is reprinted by permission of
the publisher, Charles E. Merrill Books, Inc. "The Clergy of Barchester" was first published in *The Warden* and *Barchester Towers,* edited
and with an introduction and notes by Louis Auchincloss. Riverside
Editions B97. Copyright © 1969 by Louis Auchincloss. Reprinted by
permission of Houghton Mifflin Company.
  For additional publication information see Acknowledgments.

For Louis Lee Stanton, Jr.,
Friend and Cousin

Acknowledgments

"The Long Life and Broad Mind of Mr. Justice Holmes" and "In Search of Innocence: Henry Adams and John La Farge in the South Seas" were previously published in *American Heritage;* "The Late Jamesing of Early James" was previously published in the *Times Literary Supplement;* "Origin of a Hero" was previously published in *Afterwords,* Thomas McCormack, ed., Harper & Row, Publishers, Inc. The following pieces appeared first in somewhat different form in the publications listed after their titles: "Marcel Proust: The Autobiography in the Novel," "Nancy Mitford's Versailles," "Lytton Strachey: The Last Elizabethan," and "Saint-Simon: Novelist or Historian?" in the *New York Times Book Review;* "Jane Austen and the Good Life" in *Persuasion,* Limited Editions Club; "Dreiser's Love of America" in *Sister Carrie,* Merrill Standard Edition; and "The Clergy of Barchester" in *The Warden and Barchester Towers,* Riverside Edition, Houghton Mifflin Company. A section of "Swann, Male Chauvinist and Albertine, Boy-Girl" appeared in the *New York Times.*

Contents

Life, Law
and Letters

The Long Life and Broad Mind
of Mr. Justice Holmes

F EW MEN have seen as much of our history, and from
such advantageous viewpoints, as Oliver Wendell Holmes,
Jr. As a boy in Massachusetts he met veterans of the Revolution. He went to school in a Boston shaken by abolition. He
fought through the Civil War, and it is said to have been his
voice that shouted the rough warning to Lincoln when the
President exposed his high hat above the ramparts at Fort
Stevens. With peace Holmes became a lawyer and a great
scholar. He served as a judge for half a century, first on the
high bench of Massachusetts and then on the United States
Supreme Court. And at the age of ninety-two, just retired,
he received an early official visit from the newly elected
Franklin D. Roosevelt. ("Why are you reading Plato, Mr.
Justice?" was the President's genial opening.) That such a
span of life should have been granted to a man so competent
to use it is a rare event in the history of any nation.

Holmes was born in 1841 in Boston, into a world that regarded itself as the intellectual and commercial center of the
nation. His father, Dr. Oliver Wendell Holmes, was not only
one of America's favorite poets and novelists; he was also a

distinguished medical practitioner who published a paper on
the contagiousness of puerperal fever which saved the lives of
thousands, perhaps millions, of women. On his mother's side
the infant was a grandson of Justice Charles Jackson of the
Supreme Judicial Court of Massachusetts, on which bench
Holmes was later to sit not only as an associate, but as chief
justice.

The Holmeses were not rich, but they were comfortably
off. Dr. Holmes, a wit and a raconteur, was in high demand
at intellectual gatherings. Charles Sumner, Emerson, and
Longfellow were close friends and frequent callers at his
house. Such a background has been regarded by many as a
check to the creative impulse. Henry Adams, born three
years before Oliver Wendell Holmes, Jr., under the very
shadow of the State House, claimed that he had been less
equipped for life in nineteenth-century America than if he
had started as a polish Jew, "a furtive Yacoob and Ysaac
still reeking of the Ghetto, snarling a weird Yiddish to the
officers of the customs." Holmes, however, had little use for
such self-dramatization. He selected from his background
what tools he needed for the life that he wished to lead, and
discarded the rest as best he could. He grew up into a tall,
lean, strong young man, strikingly handsome yet of a cool
disposition, tolerant, amused, incessantly curious, but with a
certain disdain for the mob and an iron determination to
lead his life by his own lights no matter what people or forces
might stand in his way.

He was one of eighty in the Harvard class of 1861, graduat-
ing just as the Civil War began. Although he was repelled by
what he saw as the excesses of the abolitionists and although
he was always fond of many Southerners, there was no question in his mind but that the Union had to be preserved, and
he enlisted at once in the Twentieth Massachusetts Regi-

ment, known as the "Harvard Regiment," in which he was soon commissioned. Many of the intellectuals of his generation, including Henry and William James, did not take up arms in the war. Holmes did not seem particularly critical of such men. He believed that each man should make up his own mind. During his three years' service, he was three times badly wounded: in the chest at Ball's Bluff, in the neck at Antietam, and in the heel at Fredericksburg.

After Antietam the enthusiastic and emotional Dr. Holmes rushed to his son's side, taking care to record the dramatic events of his journey in an article for the *Atlantic Monthly,* "My Hunt After 'The Captain.' " The son noted this, as he also noted his father's undoubted affection. He was always just, but his father's florid style was not to be his. As he later said, the Harvard Regiment never wrote about itself in a newspaper.

Holmes always regarded his military service as the most intensely lived part of his existence. In later years when commercial greed seemed to engulf America, he was to feel that the long absence of the cruel test of warfare was making people soft. On the whole, although he admired men like the railroad tycoon James J. Hill, whom he regarded as representing "one of the greatest forms of human power," he preferred warriors to stockbrokers. And in a Memorial Day address at Harvard in 1895 he made a statement which today sounds remarkably bellicose: "War, when you are at it, is horrible and dull. It is only when time has passed that you see that its message was divine . . . For high and dangerous action teaches us to believe as right beyond dispute things for which our doubting minds are slow to find words of proof. Out of heroism grows faith in the worth of heroism. The proof comes later, and even may never come. Therefore I rejoice at every dangerous sport which I see pursued.

The students at Heidelberg, with their sword-slashed faces, inspire me with sincere respect. I gaze with delight upon our polo players. If once in a while in our rough riding a neck is broken, I regard it, not as a waste, but as a price well paid for the breeding of a race fit for headship and command."

In light of the above, the way that his own military career ended may seem curious. The Twentieth Regiment had been enlisted for three years, and Holmes was entitled to be discharged in the summer of 1864. In July of that year, when the war had still eight of its bloodiest months to run, he resigned his commission and returned to Boston to study law. But Holmes never sought excuses, and he insisted in this as in all his other actions, on his individual prerogative. Here is what he wrote his parents:

I started this thing as a boy. I am now a man and I have been coming to the conclusion for the last six months that my duty has changed. I can do a disagreeable thing or face a great danger coolly enough when I *know* it is a duty — but a doubt demoralizes me as it does any nervous man — and I honestly think the duty of fighting has ceased for me — ceased because I have laboriously and with much suffering of mind and body *earned* the right . . . to decide for myself how I can best do my duty to myself, to the country, and, if you choose, to God.

As an old man Holmes came to question the validity of this decision. But it was certainly consistent with his concept of independence. He never shrank before the enemy, nor did he shrink before the prospect of what his family and friends might think of his packing up and going home before Richmond had been taken. Certainly he never regarded this decision as qualifying his right to extol the military virtues to youth.

After Harvard Law School, Holmes was admitted to the Massachusetts bar in 1867. He practiced for a short time with his brother, Edward Jackson Holmes, and then joined the firm that became known as Shattuck, Holmes & Munroe, the Boston partnership with which his name has been predominantly associated. He had a general practice, with considerable litigation, but his great passion was exploring the origins of law to establish a theoretical basis for fundamental legal doctrine. In the course of the decade and a half before his appointment to the bench, Holmes dedicated most of his nights and weekends to this scholarship. Thus, even as a busy lawyer, he was able to edit the twelfth edition of Kent's *Commentaries on American Law* in 1873, and in 1881, just before his fortieth birthday, he brought out his own enduring classic, *The Common Law*.

These years of law practice and scholarship constitute a rather arid period in the history of Holmes's personality. The man who in 1897 could write to a friend of the divinity of vitality, the wonderful capability of complex and civilized man to "lark like a boy," is scarcely perceptible in the midnight toiler. Yet this was also the period of his marriage, at thirty-one, to Fanny Dixwell, a few months older than himself, daughter of the headmaster of the school he had attended in preparation for Harvard. Mrs. Holmes, who lived almost as long as her husband, had a character that is difficult to piece out. Her complete devotion to Holmes has always been recognized. But she was a shy woman of few or no intimates. She was an efficient housekeeper, a serious artist in needlepoint, and a woman of strong will, few words, and sharp wit. Her adoration of her husband was probably intensified by the childlessness of their marriage, and she never interfered either with his work or with his pleasures. For example, she rarely accompanied him on his summer trips to England, giving as her excuse her dislike of the Atlantic voyage. But I suspect that she knew how much he loved the intellectual companionship of his English friends and felt that she was a drag on such expeditions.

Holmes and his wife lived at first with his parents, which could not have been easy for Fanny. That he must have considerably neglected her, working so intently, there can be little doubt. In the opinion of William James, at that time one of his best friends, all of Holmes's noble qualities were poisoned by "cold blooded, conscious egotism and conceit," and William's mother, writing to her novelist son Henry in England, said of him: "His whole life, soul and body, is utterly absorbed in his last work [the Kent *Commentaries*]."

Henry James was more perceptive than his brother. He was always one to appreciate the necessary loneliness of hard work, and he recognized in early youth that Holmes was destined to a great success, although "in a speciality." In later years Holmes visited Henry James on trips to England, and the latter perceived that the former's personality never essentially changed. Henry speculated that this quality of being inalterable might spring from a failure to live. This may seem a strange comment to be made about a warrior and a busy judge by a fussy old literary bachelor who had avoided military service in the Civil War, but its significance will be appreciated by those critics who have found in Holmes's Olympian detachment a suggestion of occasional heartlessness, or at least indifference, to his fellow man. Henry put it more agreeably when he described Holmes as moving through life "like a full glass carried without spilling a drop."

James Bradley Thayer, who collaborated with Holmes in the editing of Kent's *Commentaries,* felt that Holmes had treated him badly in arrogating to himself most of the credit, and Charles W. Eliot, the president of Harvard, was indignant when Holmes in 1882 resigned a professorship, which he had just accepted at the Law School, to accept the governor's appointment to the Supreme Judicial Court of Massachusetts. But on Holmes's side it must be pointed out that he indeed had done the major work on the *Commentaries,* and that he had written a letter to President Eliot when he accepted the Harvard appointment, reserving the privilege to resign it if appointed to any judicial post.

It seems, on balance, that Holmes's friends were severe on him in this period. He had to support himself, and he would have had to give up his greatest goal in life had he not used every available minute for hard work. He was not a man of overweening ambition, but when it was a question of those things about which he cared, such as the credit for a book that he had largely written, or the acceptance of a judicial post that might never be offered again, he could act with a speed and determination that may have had an air of ruthlessness. Once Holmes was convinced that what he was doing was the right thing, judged entirely by his own standards, he did not give a damn what anyone else thought.

Holmes, in *The Common Law,* explored the origins of civil and criminal liability in Anglo-Saxon, German, and Roman law. His famous statement, on the very first page, that the life of the law has not been logic but experience, seems obvious enough today, but we must remember that he was a pioneer. He sought to articulate a theoretical basis for fundamental legal doctrine in a way that differed significantly from the attempt of many of his contemporaries to deduce legal rules from absolute principles. Such theorists had a tendency to idealize law, to see it as a constantly perfected process emanating from judicial inductions and deductions, possibly inspired, if not directed, from a higher sphere. Holmes would have none of this. Law was simply the product of history and legislation. Its substance at any given time pretty nearly corresponded with what was then "understood to be convenient."

Convenience, that was the key — convenience of the majority. Accidents were bound to happen, with damage to some, and the most convenient solution for society was to let the loss lie where it fell. Holmes points out that in early law the damaging thing could be surrendered to the plaintiff as a *total* compensation: the body of the debtor to his creditor, the biting dog to the bitten person. As civilization advanced, the debtor was allowed to buy back his body, and the owner of the dog his animal. The absolute liability of the thing became the absolute liability of its owner. Thus, initially, a moral responsibility was at the bottom of the defendant's liability to pay. He had owned the offending thing at his peril.

Holmes now embarks on the development of his great thesis: that the development of law is, in the last analysis, the transmutation of this moral standard into an external one. Society may start with moral responsibility, but that is soon found to be practically inadequate. Actual intent cannot be the test; it must be *imputed* to persons who behave in a certain way:

A man who intentionally sets fire to his own house, which is so near to other houses that the fire will manifestly endanger them, is guilty of arson if one of the other houses is burned in consequence. In this case, an act which would not have been arson, taking only its immediate consequences into account, becomes arson by reason of more remote consequences which were manifestly likely to follow, whether they were actually intended or not.

This is true, as Holmes proceeds to establish, in civil as well as criminal liability. The law frequently penalizes, or forces to pay, "those who have been guilty of no moral wrong and who could not be condemned by any standard that did not avowedly disregard the personal peculiarities of the individuals concerned." Under the common law, a man acts at his peril. But it would have been going too far for courts to hold a man responsible for all the consequences of his acts. He was only responsible for the *foreseeable* consequences, not those that he had actually foreseen but those which a prudent man (as defined by a judge or jury) *would* have foreseen. Thus, conduct that is criminal or tortious is conduct that the average member of the community would regard as such. Such conduct we must all avoid, or pay the damages or be jailed or even hanged. But "the tests of liability are external, and independent of the degree of evil in the particular person's motives or intentions."

Holmes rode his horse of the external standard a bit hard through other fields of law. He seemed intent on obliterating the entire question of morality. In contracts he argued that there was no duty on the part of a promisor to perform, but simply an election to choose between performance and the payment of damages. And a "right," he claimed, was nothing but a prophecy: a prognostication that society would back one up if one took such and such a stand. In later years he liked to quote his old professor at Harvard, Louis Agassiz, who had said that in parts of Germany there would be a revolution if one added two cents to the cost of a glass of beer.

Presumably, the privilege to buy beer at a certain rate had become a right in that place and time.

If one were to assess *The Common Law* today as a work of legal history, it might receive only indifferent marks. The texts available to Holmes in the 1870s were often corrupt. The Anglo-Saxon material, for example, began to reach definitive form only three decades later. Yet the book still remains important for its expression of legal theory. His conception of the external standard has had its logical consequence in our modern tendency to eliminate guilt from liability, as seen in workmen's compensation laws and in no-fault automobile insurance.

I have dwelt at some length on *The Common Law* because I believe that it represents the culmination of Holmes's immersion in matters intellectual. For the next fifty years he was too busy a judge to write books, but he never changed his fundamental views from those stated in 1881. Idealists have attacked his materialism. Is there not an implication in his legal philosophy that moral standards have no place even in the realm of the conscience? Has a man no obligation to his neighbor but what the average citizen conceives as such? Can morality be reduced to simple good manners? And is a good deed good even if directed by an evil motive? Or a bad deed bad even if directed by a good one? Did Holmes not reject all religion?

He was, it was true, an agnostic, perhaps an atheist. He never considered that man was central, or even necessarily important, to the cosmos. He did not believe in a life after death. When his wife died, it took the persuasion of his brothers on the court, apprehensive of the scandal of such godlessness in high places, to induce him to have any funeral service at all. But there was never any question of his own moral standards. He may have laughed at himself for being the heir to a puritan background, but he did not kick against its restraints. He had a deep sense of the importance of being a gentleman — in the best sense of that word — even in a cold and indifferent universe. How can rational men be Christians? he asked Sir Frederick Pollock, the eminent British legal authority, and here is how he answered his own question: "It is like the justification of conventions — I respect a tall hat or the cult of monogamy not from the internal self-satisfaction of the accidents of space and time but from the consideration that the inward necessity of man to idealize must express itself in inadequate and transitory symbols of no value in themselves but reverent for the eternal movement of which they are the momentary form."

Holmes's work on the Supreme Judicial Court of Massachusetts represented a highly creative period in the development of law, and he came to be a leading, if not the dominant, figure of that bench. From the beginning, in 1882, he was happy in his new work. He loved being able to apply his knowledge in the philosophy of law to actual cases, and he found the judicial experience an exciting one. There are few positions in the world of practical affairs where a man can be so much of a scholar and a philosopher as that of judge. Holmes's life was with ideas; he had no use for facts except insofar as they gave rise inductively to general propositions. Years later, in 1919, he was to describe to Sir Frederick Pollock the feelings aroused in him by Justice Louis Brandeis's criticism of his slighting of economic statistics:

Brandeis the other day drove a harpoon into my midriff with reference to my summer occupations. He said you talk about improving your mind, you only exercise it on the subjects with which you are familiar. Why don't you try something new, study some domain of fact. Take up the textile industries in Massachusetts and after reading the reports sufficiently you can go to Lawrence and get a human notion of how it really is. I hate facts. I always say the chief end of man is to form general propositions — adding that no general proposition is worth a damn.

Holmes was an ambitious man, but his ambition lay along severely restricted lines. When his friend Henry Cabot Lodge suggested that he should run for governor of Massachusetts as a step toward becoming a senator, he replied simply, "But I don't give a damn about being senator." He said of Napoleon, "I am not interested by men whose view of life does not interest me." But he was intensely interested in judicial work and looked forward to an even larger opening than was offered by the highest bench of Massachusetts.

Washington was watching him. His reputation for liberalism stood him in good stead under the new administration of Theodore Roosevelt. Holmes's dissent in *Vegelahn* v. *Guntner* had alarmed the capitalist world, although the simple language with which he presented the conflict of capital and labor seems indisputable today:

One of the eternal conflicts out of which life is made up is that between the effort of every man to get the most he can for his services, and that of society, disguised under the name of capital, to get his services for the least possible return. Combination on the one side is patent and powerful. Combination on the other is the necessary and desirable counterpart, if the battle is to be carried on in a fair and equal way.

However, when Theodore Roosevelt appointed Holmes an associate justice of the United States Supreme Court in 1902, it was only after careful consultation with Holmes's and Roosevelt's good friend Lodge, who was then a senator. The

President was characteristically candid. He wanted to be sure that Holmes was a good party man, in entire sympathy with Roosevelt's views. Lodge was reassuring, and the appointment was made. Everything went well, from the President's point of view, until the case of *Northern Securities* v. *United States,* two years later, when Holmes dissented from the opinion of the majority, which held that the merger of the Northern Pacific and Great Northern railroads was in violation of the Sherman Antitrust Act. Holmes refused to be swept along in the wake of Roosevelt's trust busting. He pointed out that the supposed evil countered by the statute was a union between parties to exclude strangers, a combination to keep rivals out of the business and to ruin those already in it. The statute in no way prevented a combination of companies with the object of increasing the total amount of business performed. Size alone was not objectionable. If it were, he observed, either the Great Northern or the Northern Pacific might already be considered too large.

Theodore Roosevelt was irate. He made his opinion known that Holmes had truckled under to the power of big business, and exclaimed in disgust that he could carve a judge with more backbone out of a banana. It was said that he even contemplated excluding Holmes from further invitations to the White House. Holmes cared little. He always professed a liking for Theodore Roosevelt and an admiration for his way of getting things done, but he never had much respect for his intellect.

Holmes remained on the Supreme Court for thirty years, resigning when he was ninety, in 1932. Meanwhile, he and Justice Brandeis became famous for their dissents against majority opinions. It is a truism to point out that many of these dissents have since become the law. What are today regarded the fundamental rights of workers and unions were long denied because of the judicial doctrine of the sacredness of liberty of contract. Holmes had no particular predisposition toward legislative regulation of business or in favor of labor unions, but his old belief that law represented the convenience of the majority induced him to be very strongly of the opinion that legislatures must be given a wide latitude to experiment.

Dissenting from a majority opinion that denied the power to New York State to set a fifty-cent limit for the markup of theater ticket prices, Holmes said:

Lotteries were thought useful adjuncts of the State a century or so ago; now they are believed to be immoral and they have been stopped. Wine has been thought good for man from the time of the Apostles until recent years. But when public opinion changed it did not need the Eighteenth Amendment, notwithstanding the Fourteenth, to enable a State to say that business should end . . . What has happened to lotteries and wine might happen to theaters in some moral storm of the future, not because theaters were devoted to a public use, but because people had come to think that way.

He was inclined to take a more narrow look at state or federal statutes which cut down on freedom of speech. Where this occurred in time of war, he had to be convinced that there was a clear and present danger to the state in the prohibited utterance. Here, in *Abrams* v. *United States,* is one of his most eloquent arguments in favor of the "experiment" of the Constitution:

But when men have realized that time has upset many fighting faiths, they may come to believe even more than they believe the very foundations of their own conduct that the ultimate good desired is better reached by free trade in ideas — that the best test of truth is the power of the thought to get itself accepted in the competition of the market, and that truth is the only ground upon which their wishes safely can be carried out. That, at any rate, is the theory of our Constitution. It is an experiment, as all life is an experiment. Every year if not every day we have to wage our salvation upon some prophecy based upon imperfect knowledge. While that experiment is part of our system I think that we should be eternally vigilant against attempts to check the expression of opinions that we loathe and believe to be fraught with death, unless they so imminently threaten immediate interference with the lawful and pressing purposes of the law that an immediate check is required to save the country.

The rather fuzzy, sentimentalized picture of Holmes, developed by the great claque of his admirers in his old age, as a persistently fighting liberal, always on the side of the underdog, can be misleading. Holmes was first and foremost a judge. Because he did not think it proper for a court to weigh the wisdom of a statute and to superimpose upon a legislature the court's own economic or social predilections, he was inclined to sustain rather than throw out new laws. As a good percentage of such laws during his long tenure on the Supreme Court tended toward the restraint and regulation of big industry, he is sometimes thought to have been in favor of a regulated society. Yet in his correspondence he again and again denies any such predisposition.

He scoffed at socialism, claiming that "the crowd" already had pretty much of the national wealth and asserting that the palaces and yachts of the rich amounted only to a drop in the bucket. He repeatedly expressed his admiration for the giants of industry who seemed to strike him as bigger men than do-gooders and uplifters. And more than once, in defending free speech in his correspondence, he said that it was the right "of a fool to drool." Once even, in a moment of impatience, he exclaimed to the lady sitting next to him at din-

ner that he "loathed" most of the things that he decided in
favor of.

There were times, indeed, when Holmes struck some of his
contemporaries as the very reverse of liberal. He regretted the
prosecution by the government of cases against antiwar prop-
agandists, but he sustained its right to bring them, and after
the *Debs* decision a package addressed to him with a bomb
was intercepted in the post office. He defended the right of
the state of Washington to prosecute the publishers of a
pamphlet celebrating the glories of nudism because it en-
couraged "a disrespect for the law," and in *Baily* v. *Alabama*
he dissented from the majority opinion and argued the con-
stitutionality of an Alabama statute (the so-called Negro
peonage law) that made a worker's refusal to perform labor
as agreed presumptive evidence of an intent to defraud the
employer. Holmes here refused to admit the climate of local
prejudice:

We all agree that this case is to be considered and decided in the
same way as if it arose in Idaho or New York. Neither public
document nor evidence discloses a law which, by its administration, is made something different from what it appears on its
face, and therefore the fact that in Alabama it mainly concerns
the blacks does not matter . . .

But the opinions just cited are intended only to demonstrate
the variety of his thinking. If he loathed some of the things
he decided for, it must be remembered that he also loved de-
ciding things that he loathed. He knew that the law could
only develop healthily in the way that it had always developed — as a combination of history and legislation, and that
for such development judicial restraint was essential. Justice
Felix Frankfurter, who succeeded Benjamin Cardozo, who

succeeded Holmes, was Holmes's closest disciple in this philosophy, and lived to see his principles discredited by liberals.

Holmes was always an omnivorous reader. Books seemed to provide him with a life that was as necessary as his work on the Court. Again and again in his letters we find him yearning for the summer vacation at Beverly Farms, when he would be able to read all day. His list of titles is so long and various that it is hard to make many generalizations about it, but one may note a primary interest in current books by philosophers of law, history, and science. Holmes wanted to know every possible theory of man's role in the cosmos. Yet he was always willing to try any other work that a trusted fellow reader suggested, and his efforts in this respect were nothing if not thorough. We see him, for example, plunging into the famous French critic Sainte-Beuve at the suggestion of British political scientist Harold Laski and not really much enjoying the experiment, yet refusing to give up until he had read fourteen volumes of the *Causeries du Lundi* and all of that mammoth work, *Port-Royal*. He read fiction with less enthusiasm but with considerable insights. He admired the young Ernest Hemingway with reservations, and Willa Cather without them. He read Alfred North Whitehead and Morris Cohen and Bertrand Russell and Oswald Spengler — and also Milt Gross and Anita Loos.

His wide reading brings one inevitably to his correspondence, which is closely bound up with it. Five volumes of this have now been published, including the Holmes-Pollock letters and the Holmes-Laski letters. Holmes and Sir Frederick Pollock were contemporaries and lifelong friends, and both were legal scholars, philosophers, and aristocrats. Both were reserved, independent, strong-minded men. In the correspondence, which covers nearly sixty years, their minds met on every kind of legal, political, social, or literary problem. The letters make fascinating reading even for those not versed in law.

Holmes's letters to Harold Laski are a bit less interesting. Laski was a generation younger and treated his correspondent with marked deference. Holmes was very fond of him, but he was inclined to use him as a literary retriever. He wanted the names of all the books Laski was reading, and he was supplied with a feast. Yet he did not always, as with Pollock, follow up on topics that Laski evidently wished to discuss. At rare moments, however, Holmes would let himself go in a bit of natural description. One can only wish that there were more of such passages as the following: "The event of the week has been the opening of the Freer Gallery in the Smithsonian grounds — a beautiful building — with a square in the middle a patch of green, a little fountain and two peacocks and a peahen. The lady it is said will have nothing to do with one of them and he flocked apart and took the sunlight. The other displayed his fan and shivered with amorous anticipations."

Fanny Holmes died in 1929 at the age of eighty-nine, and Holmes wrote to his friends that she had made life poetry for him. He said that he was glad that she had gone first, for he felt — and one is sure correctly — that she would have been worse off without him than he without her. It was only too evident that he had constituted her entire life, whereas she had hardly expected — or even wanted — to constitute all of his. In the following year Charles Evans Hughes was appointed chief justice, and Holmes wrote to Laski that he had lunched at the White House, and that Mrs. Hoover had told him that the President would have liked to appoint him but had thought that he should not be burdened. Indeed, he did not want the appointment; he no longer cared for anything that anyone could give him. On January 12, 1931, he retired from the Court. Harvard Law School continued to send him one of its brightest graduates each year, to be his law clerk and secretary, until his death in 1935, just before his ninety-fourth birthday.

In the final years Holmes became a national hero and was inundated, almost to the point of asphyxiation, with laudations. His fame extended far beyond the legal field, and he was elevated to a kind of old national darling to thousands who could not have understood a page of *The Common Law*. Holmes's attitude about this outburst of fame was amiable enough, but he was never one to value highly any praise that was not discriminating. A word of approval from Sir Frederick Pollock was worth a thousand hosannas. His life had been a happy one, because he had had his chance and had used it, the chance to break his heart "in trying to make every word living and real." The only tragedy would have been to have missed it, a thought which had haunted him in the long campaigns of the Civil War. He never forgot the friends of the Twentieth Regiment who had lost their chances at Ball's Bluff, or Antietam, or Fredericksburg.

Origin of a Hero

F ROM MY twelfth to my eighteenth year I was a student at
Groton School, an institution then approaching the end
of the fifty-five-year administration of its veteran headmaster
and founder, Endicott Peabody. Dr. Peabody had, more than
any person I have ever known, the quality that military men
like to describe as "command presence." He was not only
physically large and imposing; his character and personality
were sustained by a vibrant religious faith that, so far as I
know, was never clouded by a doubt. He had been educated
in England where his father had been the London representative of the Morgan Bank, and he seemed to belong more
to the nineteenth century than to the twentieth. As a headmaster, he was in the tradition of Arnold of Rugby whose
revolutionary idea of a church school had been that the
church should be first and foremost.

In those years my imagination was at its most impression-
able, and it was utterly engrossed by a school where I was at
first abysmally wretched and later moderately content, and
where at first I did everything badly and ultimately a few
things well. Sooner or later I knew that it was bound to provide me with material for the fiction that I had started writing as early as fourteen. And indeed in later years I did begin

to write of schoolboys, but I always reserved the subject of a headmaster for the time when I should feel ready to handle it. I already had an inkling that it was going to be my major theme.

What troubled me most was the personality of Dr. Peabody, which for a long time massively blocked my embryonic story. Of course, many of the Groton family are convinced to this day that my Rector of Justin, F ancis Prescott, was modeled directly on Dr. Peabody. This kind of identification among a writer's acquaintances is inevitable, and, as one member of the Peabody family told me, it showed how little people remembered him. My difficulty with the shade of Dr. Peabody was not that I was unwilling to use him as a protagonist, but that I *could* not. His character had been too simple and too direct for my purposes. I had become convinced that the central problem in all New England Protestant church schools of his day was the conflict between the piety and idealism of their inspirers and the crass materialism of the families from which they drew not only their students but their endowments. I found some evidence that Dr. Peabody, in his retirement, had come to a troubled awareness of this dichotomy; but during the bulk of his active life I am sure that, beyond a mild disappointment that so few of his graduates went into the church and so many to the stock market, he was happily unconscious of how far his reach had exceeded his grasp.

Furthermore, he had never been an intellectual man; he had never quite trusted the arts. He had seemed to think that they were like tobacco or alcohol, all right if not taken in excess. He once protested that his boys wasted their time in Christmas vacations at the theater because they were more interested in the "pulchritude" of the actresses than in the message of the play, but as one acute graduate pointed

out, Dr. Peabody himself would have been the first to look
askance at the boy who was more interested in the message
than the actress. In my youth I had been a passionate ad-
mirer of Dr. Peabody, but I could not acclimatize myself as
a mature novelist to the prospect of a fictional headmaster
who would be unmoved by Jane Austen or Balzac and who
might have even raised his eyebrows at the sublime sonnets
of Shakespeare.

No, to dramatize the troubled story of the Protestant
church school my headmaster would have to be a much more
complicated character than Endicott Peabody. He would
have to have moments of doubt to balance his faith; he
would have to see his school as a mountain of vanity as well
as a monastery; he would have to be intellectual, cultivated,
occasionally cynical, sometimes cruel, always clever. If Dr.
Peabody had his moments of despair, they didn't show. I
wanted my man to be tortured in his brilliant success by constantly having to question its validity, and at times to despise
even his own teachers and pupils for their failure to make his
ideals seem as shining as he had aspired to make them. I
wanted him to be humble and vain, to be St. Francis of Assisi
and King Lear on the heath. I wanted him to express the
agony of failing ridiculously when he wanted at the very
least to fail magnificently, and I wanted him to raise the
question — no more than that — if he had failed at all.

The greatest man whom I ever had the good luck to know
was the late Judge Learned Hand. He offered here and there
a clue to what I wanted, and in the final characterization of
my Francis Prescott I put in more than one of his traits. I
even inserted a couple of stories that he had told me, but
when the novel appeared, this was noticed by only one of my
correspondents. I might parenthetically make the suggestion
to incipient novelists that, if they wish to disguise a character

drawn in any part from life, all they need do is change his profession. To most readers the word "fiction" is an utter fraud. They are entirely convinced that each character has an exact counterpart in real life and that any small discrepancy with that counterpart is a simple error on the author's part. Consequently, they are totally at a loss if anything essential is altered. Make Abraham Lincoln a dentist, put the Gettysburg Address on his tongue, and nobody will recognize it.

As I began gradually to make out my headmaster, I began also dimly to discern my school. It would have to be more characteristic than special; it would have to be large, more like St. Paul's than like Groton, and have a dash of English public school toughness, for the eastern seaboard, at the end of the last century, was inclined to be Anglophile. It would have to embrace the best, and some of the worst, aspects of the New England Protestant church schools, and, most importantly of all, it would have to arouse in the reader a genuine question as to whether the education that it provided for boys was more of an asset than a liability.

It was my hope that I would be able to remain impartial about this question, as it seemed to me that I was evenly divided in my heart as to whether my own education had done me more good or harm. But I was perfectly clear that, to balance existing trends of thought, defense would be more needed than attack. To hit the Groton of my day would be to beat a dead horse. The educational concept of secluding a group of boys from the temptations of the world while they are inculcated with physical and mental discipline in the ambience of a single faith has become hopelessly unfashionable. Regardless of what I felt about my own school, I would have to do a good bit of explaining of any similar institution if I did not want its goals to seem merely foolish to contemporary readers.

Similarly, with my headmaster, I would have to explain the value of his inspirational qualities to some boys as well as their almost murderous effect on others. When the book was ultimately published, I ran into a good deal of comment in the press as to whether or not I "approved" of my headmaster. I don't know. Certainly I considered him a great man, and I meant that his faith should be as much the core of the novel as the faithlessness of Saul Bellow's protagonist is that of *Herzog*. Surely, it is as valid to study faith as to study its absence, particularly in delineating institutions founded on it. But I suppose there is no getting away from the old business of "taking sides." There are still people who claim that Shylock is a hero and others who maintain him to be a villain. In our era, it may be permissible for a novelist to be neutral about an alienated character or a nonhero, but if he introduces the values of yesteryear, he is expected to show where he stands. However, in this respect, as in many others, the Goncourt brothers remain my models. I am neither a satirist nor a cheerleader. I am strictly an observer.

My next problem was how to tell my story. It would have to cover a considerable lifetime, for reading through all the biographies that I could find of New England headmasters (a dreary task), I was struck by how many had attained longevity. Furthermore, there seemed to be one generation that had obviously been the "great" generation, that of Peabody, Drury, Thayer, and Mather, a generation of thunderous idealists and of long reigns; and it was clearly among this little group of splendid contemporaries that I would have to place my protagonist if my story was to achieve the proper verisimilitude. The only way I could see to deal with the problem of a long-lived character was to cast the novel in the form of a biography, or even of an autobiography.

I rejected the idea of autobiography, for the simple reason that one of the most important aspects of any headmaster is his effect, presumably powerful, on other people. This even a fictional autobiographer cannot very well describe without seeming fatuous. Then I was afraid that doing the book in the form of a biography would limit me to the point of view of my fictional biographer, but I found that I could get around this by the expedient of introducing the reader to my biographer's source material, so that he would be constantly looking over the latter's shoulder as he put together his book. This opened up a wide field for the proliferation of points of view. My biographer would be able to ask people who had known the headmaster to write up for him some particular period of the headmaster's life. He could find letters and diaries which would be set forth in full in the manuscript, or he could record his own conversations with persons who had interesting memories of his subject. Of course, I ran here into the danger of having the finished book seem artificial. There are some critics who will always attack a literary device of this sort, whether or not it be successfully executed. They will arbitrarily refuse to understand why any character who is telling them a story should be telling them that particular story and should be telling it to them in those words. But to me it always seemed that to tell a tale through an "I" is one of the most basic and natural forms of storytelling, and the gulf between myself and the critics who feel it must be apologized for is an unbridgeable one.

Actually, even from a strictly factual point of view, I discovered, after finishing *The Rector of Justin,* that nothing which my fictional biographer had turned up could not have been turned up by a true biographer writing a book about a true headmaster. One friend sent me a privately published diary, several hundred pages in length, that had been kept by a master at a boys' boarding school for the purpose of recording, over the decades, his secret but never-diminishing detestation of a very famous headmaster.

But my fictional biographer, what sort of a man was he to be? I was caught up for a while by a fancy theory that intrigued and later almost obsessed me of a man who would be convinced that the headmaster had been a saint, a true saint in the orthodox Christian sense. As one read his book, however, it would somehow have to become clear to the reader, in Jamesian fashion, that the saint was not, indeed, the headmaster, whose worldliness and occasional cruelty barred him from any such category, but the biographer himself. This was not only a theme that I found I could not handle; it turned out to be a theme that had no true relation to my point of departure. It was another book altogether. I then decided that my biographer should be an early graduate of the school, a poor boy who later made a fortune and became chairman of its board of trustees. He would raise the huge sums needed for the school's endowment and bring Mammon onto the hitherto innocent campus. Needless to say, he would be loathed by the headmaster. I eventually did put such a character into the book, and he played a leading role as David Griscam; but the first version of the novel, in which he appeared as the headmaster's biographer, had to be scrapped entirely when his personality got out of hand.

A week after giving up this first draft, when I was absolutely discouraged, I had a sudden inspiration of how the book should be done.

My biographer would be a man two generations younger than the headmaster, who would make his first appearance at the end of the old man's life. The headmaster would be attracted to him by the one quality that they had in common: their religious faith. To make this stronger I would define my biographer in terms of opposites to the headmaster. He would be unhealthy, irresolute, untidy, utterly devoid of "command presence." He would be sensitive and emotional, yet redeemed by integrity and courage. He would become the intimate of the headmaster because they would both come to realize that the faith which was the bond between them was almost totally lacking in the school, the faculty, the parents, and the trustees. These latter all would care only about the appearance of faith. Indeed, they would often be actually antagonistic to anything *but* this appearance. As Brian Aspinwall (which was my biographer's name) and Dr. Prescott would come to recognize what they had in common and its tragic uniqueness in the world about them, they would be drawn together in love and in despair. Brian, after the death of Dr. Prescott, would be able to live only in his planned biography.

The form of the book, then, was not going to be a biography but a preparation for a biography. It would be cast in the form of Brian Aspinwall's journal starting in 1939 with his first meeting of Dr. Prescott, and ending in 1946 just after the latter's death, when Brian decides to start his book about him. At each point in the journal where he comes upon material shedding light on the life of Dr. Prescott, that material is included in chronological order. On the last page Brian has completed his researches and, as the reader closes the book, Brian is picking up his pencil to start his biography. We never know, therefore, what he writes or even if he succeeds in writing it. Personally, I doubt if Brian would have been able to finish it. As I see him, he is the kind of perfectionist who would be constantly tearing up each page that he had written.

Besides Brian Aspinwall, I decided to add, in the form of material he discovers or collects, the points of view of five other observers. An old expatriate dandy, an epicure and life-long friend of Dr. Prescott, gives Brian three unpublished chapters of his never-to-be-published memoir, "The Art of Friendship," dealing with Dr. Prescott's youth. Brian then gets his material for the early years of the school through the notes supplied him by David Griscam, the embittered would-be biographer of Dr. Prescott, who has abandoned his project because of the headmaster's hostility. He learns of the domestic side of the headmaster's life through his talks with Dr. Prescott's daughter and through reading a chapter of a novel written by her lover who has died of World War I injuries. And finally, Brian sees the memoir written by Mr. Griscam's son, who has committed suicide, as an exercise for a French psychiatrist who was attempting to exorcise from his patient's soul the ghost of the headmaster whom he had hated in his boyhood.

Once I had my scheme, after so much floundering, the book was speedily written. It still seems to me that the shifting points of view are successful in keeping constantly open the question of good or evil in the headmaster's relationships. What to me is not meant to be open is the central fact of his faith and sincerity. And so, in the end, perhaps I did what I had first had in mind: to write a work of hagiography, to study a saint and to leave it up to the reader whether saints are good or bad.

Emily Dickinson:
The Private Publication

MANY ASPECTS of Emily Dickinson's life have fascinated her readers of our era, but none more than her reluctance to publish her poetry. As her fame continues to rise and our own personal reticences to diminish, this reluctance strikes us as more and more curious. In an age when reports of the stools of ill presidents are subject to national scrutiny, when noted public figures discuss their sex lives on television, when it is no shame to admit publicly one's alcoholism or drug addiction, the refusal of a writer to share with us her lyrics on such general subjects as death, immortality, and love seems bizarre, to say the least.

But writers have not always felt it necessary to communicate beyond the limit of those whom they could see or hear. Homer, we may surmise, was satisfied to recite his epics. Shakespeare produced his plays and acted in them, but, so far as we can tell, he was printed in his lifetime only in pirated quartos or in order to forestall pirated quartos. John Donne was content to hand copies of his verses to friends.

Nearer to our own day, Gerard Manley Hopkins sought only the opinion of a few selected friends as to the merits of his poetry.

Emily Dickinson, contrary to a popular impression, was not content to write verses for herself alone. As soon as she had written a poem that she thought had merit she needed to have it read. She wanted it to be seen by a member of the small appreciative circle of her family and close friends. Several hundred poems were thus transmitted in letters. Her trust was justified by the care with which these were kept. She lived in an age when people kept letters. *That,* to her, was publication enough.

Nonetheless, many critics have believed that she was desperately frustrated, that she was held back from publishing by shyness, fear of failure, dread of exposure, or possibly simply by the negative attitude of Thomas Wentworth Higginson. Yet there is no evidence in her letters of such frustration. Never does she give expression to any violent feeling, any professed horror at the idea of publicity, such as one might expect from a person racked between lust for fame and fear of the limelight. Even when a poem of hers actually appeared in a paper or book, submitted by a friend or correspondent, with or even perhaps without her permission, she did not demonstrate the least distress. Her attitude seems to have been more one of indifference, or even of tranquil disdain. She writes to Louise Norcross in 1872 about a Miss Phelps who begged her to publish:

She wrote me in October, requesting me to aid the world by my chirrup more. Perhaps she stated it as my duty, I don't distinctly remember, and always burn such letters, so I cannot obtain it now. I replied declining.

Of course, she may not have always felt this way. A decade earlier she had written to her sister-in-law, Sue, to thank her for praising a poem. She added:

Could I make you and Austin — proud — sometime — a great way off — 'twould give me taller feet.

This would seem to imply at least a vague prognostication of literary renown, presumably through the press. And not long afterward she wrote her famous letter of April 15, 1862, to Higginson, enclosing four poems and asking him if they "breathed." When he advised her not to be in a hurry to publish, she protested that the idea was as foreign to her thought "as firmament to fin," but one wonders, had he answered more warmly, begging permission to print one or all of the four in the *Atlantic Monthly,* if she would have refused. When an author writes to a famous editor out of the blue, there must be at least a consideration of the possibility of being printed. But even this does not mean that publication was important to Emily Dickinson. It was at the most, I submit, an idea with which she toyed and which Higginson's qualified admiration helped to quash under her more characteristic diffidence. Only a year later her attitude was less equivocal, as expressed in her best known statement on the subject:

> *Publication — is the Auction*
> *Of the Mind of Man —*
> *Poverty — be justifying*
> *For so foul a thing.*

Some critics have argued that she may have distinguished here between *giving* her poems to the public and selling

them, but I see nothing in this. Even if she had given a poem
to Higginson, he would still have sold it. What she calls the
"disgrace of price" would have equally marked the trans-
action.

In later years Emily Dickinson became firm enough in her
attitude to resist even the strongest appeals to publish of her
friend Helen Hunt Jackson. She made only one exception,
when she gave Mrs. Jackson "Success is Counted Sweetest"
for an anthology. But that she was more indifferent to the
press than hostile or fearful is borne out by the fact that she
did not bother to protest the liberties taken by the editor in
the final version of the poem.

Confining her audience to a small group was perfectly
consistent with the self-imposed limitations of Emily Dickinson's life. She reacted so intensely to experiences that she
could afford few beyond those offered by her immediate environment. She had always to be eliminating persons and
places. First, Massachusetts was too big; then Amherst; finally her house and garden were world enough. A handful of
friends sufficed for her heart; a handful of readers for her
poems. It was not so much that she shrank from life as that
a small piece of it provided her perfervid imagination with
what it would take a world tour — or a world war — to do for
cruder souls.

It was probably difficult for Emily Dickinson even to imagine a reading public. The outside world of men and women
had little meaning to her. In the same way it was difficult for
her to take in the very existence of the Civil War. "When
did the war really begin?" she ends a letter in 1861. She tries
to put it out of mind: "I shall have no winter this year on
account of the soldiers. Since I cannot weave blankets or
boots I thought it best to omit the season." The references
to the conflict in the next four years are scanty indeed, and

one of them sounds almost callous: "A soldier called a morning ago and asked for a nosegay to take to battle. I suppose he thought we kept an aquarium." But as soon as someone she knew was killed, all the horror of war burst in on her unbearably. She deeply grieved for Frazer Stearns, "his big heart shot away by a minie ball," and sent an anguished appeal to her Norcross cousins: "Let us love better, children, it's most that's left to do."

There was great economy in Emily Dickinson's emotional life. A few deaths could make a war; a few flowers and a robin, a spring. By her own lights, she *did* publish. If her reputation today rested only on the poems sent to the Norcross sisters, Dr. and Mrs. Holland, the Bowleses, Sister Sue, and Higginson, it would still be secure. If her "neighbor" could be her "menagerie," these friends could be her public.

Living in an age of more vulgar satisfactions, I cannot help finding something attractive in Emily Dickinson's contentment with an intimate audience. There is to me an appealing humility in her concept of poetry as the product of two persons: the poet and the reader. As she writes to Louise Norcross,

It's a great thing to be "great," Loo, and you and I tug for a life, and never accomplish it, but no one can stop our looking on, and you know some cannot sing, but the orchard is full of birds, and we all can listen. What if we learn, ourselves, some day?

Even beyond the idea that poetry exists in communication to a sympathetic listener is the idea that it may exist by itself alone, like the joy that can never be in vain because it "adds to some bright total whose dwelling is unknown." Emily Dickinson, who had said that she must sing because she could not pray, came to compare herself with a bird that was indistinguishable from its own song:

I found a bird this morning, down — down — on a little bush at
the foot of the garden, and wherefore sing, I said, since nobody
hears? One sob in the throat, one flutter of bosom — "*My* business
is to *sing*"—and away she rose! How do I know but cherubim,
once, themselves, as patient, listened and applauded her unno-
ticed hymn?

This mystic sense of her own identification with the universe intensified with age. Living and poetry to her were increasingly intertwined, so that it may not be an exaggeration
to say that her life was poetry. Less and less did she need the
support of family and friends. She cared more for the dead
than the living, more for the absent than for those nearby.
Her mother, with whom she had never been close, became a
saint in the grave, and she was capable of refusing to see
friends when they called and then writing them letters to say
how much she missed them.

The letters themselves, indeed, now become bits of poems
or introductions to poems. Emily writes to Mrs. Holland, "I
must show you a bee that is eating a lilac at the window.
There — there — he is gone!" And then she breaks into:

> Bees are Black, with Gilt Surcingles —
> Buccaneers of Buzz.
> Ride abroad in ostentation
> And subsist on Fuzz.

Reading these letters, one can feel some of the relief of
the artist as she casts off the prose integument and explodes
into verse. Here is a prose letter to the Norcrosses which I
have arranged in verse lines, adding, in brackets, one article
that the rhythm seems to demand:

> Affection is like bread,
> Unnoticed till we starve.

And then we dream of it
And sing of it
And paint it,
When every urchin in the street
Has more than he can eat.
We turn not older with [the] years
But newer every day.

It was a lonely life in the end, but the compensations must have been considerable. Emily Dickinson became her own oeuvre.

Marcel Proust: The Autobiography in the Novel

PROUST IN HIS essay "La Méthode de Sainte-Beuve" vigorously attacked the great literary critic for using the external features of a writer's life and character to explain his work. He challenged Sainte-Beuve's axiom that an author's writing is inseparable from the rest of him. Proust insisted, on the contrary, that his writing is a thing apart, a secret garden that has little or nothing to do with the personality of the author observed by the world. When George Painter undertook his massive biography of Proust, with the avowed intention of seeking comprehension of *A la Recherche du Temps Perdu* in the life of its author, he had to square his mission with his subject's well-known animosity to the Sainte-Beuve method. Nor did he shirk the task.

His own approach, Painter sturdily maintained, was just the opposite of that of Sainte-Beuve, who had used a "superficial impression of an author's outward behavior" to correct "an equally superficial impression of his work." The biographer's true task, according to Painter, is to explain the two selves of a writer's being, the inner and outer, and to demonstrate their interdependence.

He must discover, beneath the mask of the author's everyday, objective life, the secret life from which he extracted his work; show how, in the apparently sterile persons and places of that external life, he found the hidden, universal meanings that are the themes of his book; and reveal the drama of the contrast and interaction between his daily existence and his incommensurably deeper life as a creator.

Now this seems to me an excellent statement of how to write a literary biography, and I believe that Painter has been successful in applying it. His book is one of a dazzling thoroughness that seems to hang every paragraph of *A la Recherche du Temps Perdu* on its appropriate biographical twig. As Proust spent a large part of his life planning and plotting the great novel that was in itself to be a kind of autobiography, the process of watching him do so through Painter's eyes has the fascination of looking at a picture in a picture in a picture.

I daresay there will be plenty to dispute some of his identifications, but, without knowing anything of the originals, I find his work totally persuasive. When Painter's footnote instructs me that it was from Comte Léon de Tinseau that Proust borrowed the monocle of General de Froberville at Mme. de Saint-Euverte's soirée, I accept it. The whole great jigsaw puzzle, with all its maps and genealogies, seems to fit to the last piece.

It is perhaps inevitable that such abundance of documentation, collated in an age when every biographer has a nodding acquaintance with the jargon of psychiatry, should tempt Painter on occasion to play God. He theorizes, for example, that Proust killed his mother twice over, first by worrying her about his health and then (after her death) by putting her furniture in a male brothel. It only remained to let her avenging spirit kill *him*. Painter ties it up neatly by identifying the dark woman of Proust's final hallucinations with the maternal murderess and ends on a sorry note of claptrap: "His novel, by leaving his deepest guilt unatoned, had led to his most terrible sin, but salvation is completed only in the material world, at the moment of forgiveness and being forgiven, which for Proust was the moment of death."

This kind of superficial packaging does little damage to the solid biographical work beneath. Seeing Proust day by day as we do in this brilliant portrait of an artist at work, we are at liberty to substitute our own amateur psychological speculations for Painter's. The real question posed by his massively detailed biography is: What is its true utility? Is it principally a contribution to the scientific investigation of the creative process or does it significantly enlarge our understanding of *A la Recherche?*

Painter's own answer is perfectly clear. He deems his book an indispensable aid in the task of comprehending Proust's work. *A la Recherche,* he states, "of all great works of art, cannot be fully understood until the life in time, of which it is a symbolic reconstruction in eternity, is known." He goes so far as to sneer at what he calls "closed system" Proustians who have been "egotistically contented" to read *A la Recherche* without relating it to the author's own life, and he concludes the preface to his biography by flinging in the nose of his still ignorant but about-to-be-illuminated reader what seems a kind of taunt: "What do they know of *A la Recherche* who only *A la Recherche* know?" The implied answer is nothing at all, or very little.

Now it is one thing to play the amusing game of tracing the originals of a novelist's characters and quite another to elevate this game to the level of indispensable literary criticism. Painter's argument seems to be that one cannot understand a portrait until one has seen the model. He will not even credit the novelist with the capacity to invent a sexual experience. He deems it "fundamental and indispensable" for the student of *A la Recherche* to know Proust's sex life, and he wets the lips of his audience with such anticipation as: "Readers who have felt all along that Proust's picture of heterosexual love is valid and founded on personal experience will be glad to find their instinct justified." Glad? Is it a parlor game with scores?

Obviously some novelists sketch closely from human models, like Proust, Thomas Wolfe, and Charlotte Brontë. In our own day Mary McCarthy has said: "What I really do is take real plums and put them in an imaginary cake." But other novelists like Emily Brontë, Henry James, and Edith Wharton, so far as one can tell, do not. In any case, whether or not they do is irrelevant to the question of their quality as novelists, for the most inferior writers can be divided into the same two categories.

I cannot see what illumination is shed on a work of fiction by even the most correct identification of the characters with models in real life. Mme. de Chevigné, Laure Hayman, Mme. Straus, Charles Haas, Bertrand de Fénelon, as seen in the pages of Painter, are like marionettes laid out on a table after a performance when compared to the living truths that Proust made of them in Oriane de Guermantes, Odette, Mme. Verdurin, Swann, and Saint-Loup. And what earthly good does it do me to know that the haunting little phrase of Vinteuil's sonata that provides the motif of Swann's love for Odette was inspired by a banal melody by Saint-Saëns, which (thanks to a purchase of the record after reading Painter) still shrieks in my ears?

I will gladly admit, however, that there is one model of Proust's who is almost as vivid in Painter's book as his counterpart in *A la Recherche*. Count Robert de Montesquiou shows all of the Baron de Charlus's wonderfully preposterous arrogance. Painter supplies a delightful anecdote that was a favorite of Proust's and that must have cost him a pang not to include in his novel. Montesquiou, having asked Maurice de Rothschild for the loan of some diamonds to wear at a fancy dress ball, was outraged to receive only a very small brooch with the warning that he should take care of it, as it was a family jewel. "I was quite unaware you had a family," Montesquiou haughtily retorted, "but I did think you might have some jewels." Charlus could not have done better!

In one respect, at least in this reader's case, Painter's painstaking research has done a small permanent damage to the appreciation of *A la Recherche*. This is in the tricky and delicate area of the identification of the narrator of the novel with Proust himself. Of course, the narrator is called "Marcel," which might seem to give the game away at the start, but it is still vital that the lens through which we see most of the episodes should be a clear one, and for this reason the narrator must remain a somewhat pale personage, without violent and distracting prejudices or preconceptions. I think that André Gide was dead wrong in trying to persuade Proust to make his narrator a sexual invert. "Marcel" should be dissociated from the homosexuality of Charlus that he describes, just as it is preferable in the sections dealing with the Dreyfus affair that he should not be Jewish. Painter himself recognizes this when he points out that, as Proust uses homosexuality, snobbism, and cruelty as symbols of universal original sin, Proust would have destroyed the "symbolic truth" of his work by making his narrator a homosexual.

Very well, but doesn't Painter destroy some of that same "symbolic truth" when he proves that Proust himself was a homosexual, a snob, and a sadist? Even conceding that Proust's own reputation for sexual inversion and social climbing is so notorious and so implicit in the text of the novel that most readers may be assumed to be on notice, there still remains the third sin, cruelty. I had never known, and would certainly not have guessed from the novel, that Proust used to pay young men to put on exhibitions in which they chased rats about a room to stick them with needles and beat them with clubs.

Now it may be squeamish of me, but I doubt that I will ever again be able to read the passages in *A la Recherche* that describe the narrator's agony at the vision of cruelty in others without accusing him in my heart of the grossest hypocrisy. Somehow I will have to learn to blot out the image of those tortured rodents to preserve the "symbolic truth" of a great work.

I do not suppose that Painter would go so far as to argue that we could not appreciate Charlotte Brontë without Elizabeth Gaskell or Scott without Lockhart or even Henry James without Leon Edel, but to distinguish Proust's case from theirs, Painter has to take him out of the category of novelists. And this is just what he does when he defines *A la Recherche* as "not properly speaking, a fiction but a creative autobiography." And what is a creative autobiography?

Proust believed, justifiably, that his life had the shape and meaning of a great work of art: It was his task to select, telescope, and transmute the facts so that their universal significance should be revealed; and this revelation of the relationship between his own life and his unborn novel is one of the chief meanings of *Le Temps Retrouvé*. But though he invented nothing, he altered everything. His places and people are composite in space and time, constructed from various sources and from widely separate periods of his life. His purpose in so doing was not to falsify reality, but on the contrary, to induce it to reveal the truths it so successfully hides in this world.

Yet what is all *that,* in the name of Richardson, Balzac, and Tolstoy, but the definition (and a very good one) of the novelist's craft? What writer's life does not, properly viewed, have the shape and meaning of a great work of art? What does Painter think novelists *do* but try to extract truth from misleading realities?

He makes one further distinction in his effort to set Proust in a separate category, and that is Wordsworth's distinction between fancy and imagination. Fancy invents and imagination interprets. Proust was indifferent to fancy but a master of imagination. Presumably we are supposed to deduce from this that it is less vital to study the life of a fanciful novelist, as his models may be presumed to be undiscoverable. But how can one be sure that Captain Ahab could not be traced, with enough psychological research, to a charwoman in Melville's New York boarding house or Clarissa Harlowe to a wax doll seen by Richardson as a child? May fancy not simply be imagination pushed a step further, and if this is true can we understand *any* novelist without doing all the work on his life that Painter has done on Proust's? Perish the thought!

All of which is not to say that the study of the creative process, of which Painter has given so splendid an example, is not a valid and instructive work. It is only to his thesis of its critical indispensability that I dissent.

The Styles of Mr. Justice Cardozo

W HEN I WENT to the University of Virginia Law
School in the fall of 1938, I was determined to turn my
back forever on the world of letters. I had failed — I had decided grimly — because my first novel, written during my jun-
ior year at Yale, had been rejected by Scribner's. It was thus
ordained, I reasoned with the violence of youth, that I should
never qualify for the exotic world of art and must resign myself to a more mundane profession. Although I thought I had
been humbled, there was still a note of then unconscious condescension in the attitude with which I approached my new
trade. It was, in the murky depths of my deepest reflections, a
second best. The world of law might have seemed to me a
more "real" world — a world, to put it crudely, more fit for
men, "real" men (whatever they were) — but it was still, to
my naiveté, inferior to the one to which I had, however
rashly, aspired.

I was in for some pleasant surprises. I soon found that the
history of English jurisprudence and the growth of the common law was quite as interesting as more general histories
that I had enjoyed at Yale. And cases in contracts, torts, and
criminal law, where judges wrestled to fit new factual situations into ancient patterns of accepted conduct, adjusting,

modifying, and sometimes making over the latter in accordance with individual theories of what "law" was or should be, fascinated me. What was a judge, describing the actions of a plaintiff or defendant in a given situation in such a way as to justify his judgment of those actions, but a novelist describing his characters so as to lend an air of verisimilitude to the moral atmosphere that he seeks to create? Perhaps I had found, like Maeterlinck's children, that the bluebird was all the while at home.

But there were aspects of the law less malleable even to an imagination as determinedly romantic as mine then was. What could it do with the flood of statute law pouring from the Congress and the state legislatures, or with the huge structure of regulations designed to interpret federal law and their appended illustrations of imagined cases where the litigants were represented by mere letters and the situations reduced to the dryest facts? Where was the possibility of drama in all of this? Where in that dreary sea of verbiage was there any prose that breathed or any detectable style? It was words, simply words, often so jumbled and obscure as to make finding the sense like hacking one's way through tangled underbrush with a machete.

The volume of such law was not then what it was to become, but the future was already marked. The masses in a world increasingly socialized were not going to allow laws affecting their daily lives to be subject to what they considered the whims of judges reared in a more individualistic society. The compulsion to legislate had already reached the point where a session of the Senate or House was labeled *good* or *bad* in accordance with the quantity of statutes passed. We were not far from the Emperor Justinian who had prohibited the judiciary from commenting on his code.

Now, of course, Justinian's effort was futile. No quantity of laws, however astutely drafted, or of regulations, however shrewdly forecast, can cover all, or even most of the situations that will arise among litigants. Judges must always exist to interpret laws. Forty years after my first term in Virginia, we have more judges, harder worked, than ever before, and in certain areas of constitutional law, notably civil rights, they are even more important. But it is still an obvious truth that when a judge's opinion may be rapidly reversed, modified, or even affirmed by a new statute or code, that opinion is going to be a less valuable precedent. As codified law, constantly modified, assimilates or rejects the decisions and opinions of the courts, these latter must become more ephemeral. We shall have no more great common law judges.

Now what is the harm of this? Probably none. I am writing subjectively. To me, a reluctant law student and a frustrated novelist, the vast, bristling black and white volume of statutory law and regulations seemed like a glacier moving ineluctably over the land to freeze below the ice the giant figures of Mansfield, Eldon, Holmes, and Cardozo, now barely discernible to the living pygmies on the surface. It was as if all my secret fears of the inevitable triumph of the philistine over the artist in our culture had been confirmed.

The figure who most helped to revive my stumbling romanticism was Benjamin Cardozo. I had seen him once on a trip to Washington when I was a boy. My father had taken me to view the Supreme Court, then sitting in the Capitol, and had pointed out the white-haired figure with the beautiful ascetic face, whispering: *"There* is the great man." One of the first books I was told to read in law school was *The Nature of the Judicial Process,* and I was immediately spellbound by a prose so formal, so majestic, so elaborate, so almost Jamesian, and yet so smooth and clear and soft. Here was a writer indeed!

I was also interested to note that he, too, was concerned that codes might "threaten the judicial function with repression and disuse and atrophy." But he did not believe that, in the long run, this would really happen. What his little book was more about was that "land of mystery" where legislation is silent and where a judge must "look to the common law for the rule that fits the case." Here indeed, as Blackstone had put it, he was the "living oracle of the law."

As I began now to study Cardozo's opinions in contracts and torts, the law became something exciting, elusive, almost mystical. It seemed to me that statutes and regulations were so much fustian of ambitious politicians and dreary bureaucrats, that we really lived in a chaos of instincts and habits and appetites and prejudices, and that law, true law (my early extravagance must be allowed), existed only in that moment when a judge fitted a particular principle to a particular set of facts, and then expired, to be remembered only in its epitaph, the judge's opinion. It was all the more important that that opinion should be beautifully constructed and expressed.

Let me try to recreate my early impressions of Cardozo by analyzing, as I saw it then, his opinion in *DeCicco* v. *Schweizer,* 221 N.Y. 431, decided by the New York Court of Appeals in 1917. No clause of a constitution or of a statute, state or federal, was here involved. The law had to be found, interpreted, and modified, by a "living oracle."

The stated facts of the case at once put me in mind of the opening of a Henry James novel. Count Oberto Gulinelli of Ferrara was engaged to be married to an American girl, presumably an heiress, one Blanche Josephine Schweizer. Her father, Joseph, evidently pleased by the prospect of this noble addition to his family, had handed his future son-in-law a written promise to pay his daughter $2500 a year after they were married. Payment was begun in 1902, immediately after the event; but in 1912 Mr. Schweizer refused to honor further his commitment. Suit was brought against him, not by his daughter or her husband, but by one DeCicco to whom the daughter had assigned her father's promise.

Alas, the romance of *The Golden Bowl* seemed already to have faded. We did not know why the father had repudiated his promise or why the daughter had sold it. The family relationship had evidently deteriorated. The fate of international marriages at the turn of the century was almost never smooth and rarely edifying.

Cardozo proceeded to review the law. It was the established rule in New York that a promise made by A to B to induce him not to break his contract with C is void because there is no consideration to support the promise. B is already under obligation to fulfill his contract with C. Mr. Schweizer had promised the Count that he would pay money to his wife if the Count carried out an engagement to which the Count was already pledged. Did not the consideration have to fail? Ah, but what if the promise had been made to B *and* C, to the Count *and* Blanche?

The writing was signed by her parents; it was delivered to her intended husband; it was made four days before the marriage; it called for a payment on the day of the marriage; and on that day payment was made, and made to her. From all these circumstances, we may infer that at the time of the marriage the promise was known to the bride as well as the husband, and that both acted upon the faith of it.

Consideration for Mr. Schweizer's promise now becomes evident. For even if the Count and Blanche were both obliged to fulfill their contract to marry, even if neither of them had the right, acting alone, to withdraw (remember that in that day a breach of a promise to marry was still actionable) , it was equally clear that, acting together, they had a right to rescind. The law had no interest in forcing two unwilling persons to wed. It was *this* right that they gave up in going to the altar on the strength of the bride's father's promise, and for this consideration the latter had now to continue to pay as he had said he would pay, even to his daughter's assignee.

But did Mr. Schweizer really intend to place such pressure on the young couple? Did he really want two reluctant persons to enter the state of matrimony for the purpose of securing a financial allowance? Cardozo said that this did not matter:

It will not do to divert the minds of others from a given line of conduct, and then to urge that because of the diversion the opportunity has gone to say how their minds would otherwise have acted. If the tendency of the promise is to induce them to persevere, reliance and detriment may be inferred from the mere fact of performance. The springs of conduct are subtle and varied. One who meddles with them must not insist upon too nice a measure of proof that the spring which he released was effective to the exclusion of all others.

And so the shabby facts, if shabby they were: the Count seeking a dowry, the sale of the promise, the dunning of the old father, were rewoven into a hard fine rule of law that seemed to embrace the situation with some of the moral beauty of *The Golden Bowl*. Cardozo went even further, too far perhaps. He reinforced his conclusion with "those considerations of public policy which cluster about contracts that touch the marriage relation." Could he really have believed that the Schweizer-Gulinelli nuptials were for the greater good of society? Or was he establishing a basis for distinguishing the case if later situations arising in the business world should make its application unjust?

I was delighted to discover that Cardozo had written an essay entitled "Law and Literature," in the very beginning of which he quoted Henry James! The great novelist was cited to support Cardozo's thesis that a judicial opinion should always be literature, that style and substance were inextricably fused in writing:

Don't let anyone persuade you (James wrote to Hugh Walpole) . . . that strenuous selection and comparison are not the very essence of art, and that form is not substance to that degree that there is absolutely no substance without it. Form alone *takes,* and holds and preserves substance, saves it from the welter of helpless verbiage that we swim in as in a sea of tasteless tepid pudding.

Cardozo then proceeded to divide the forms, or styles, or methods if you choose, of judicial opinions into six categories. He listed them as follows: the *magisterial,* where we hear "the voice of the law speaking by its consecrated ministers with the calmness and assurance that are born of a sense of mastery and power"; the *laconic* and the *conversational,* which overlap, where the homely illustration makes its way by its appeal to everyday experience and where the doubtful precept is brought down to earth and made to walk the ground; the *refined,* which, if only held back from euphuism, lends itself to cases where there is need of delicate precision; the *demonstrative,* or persuasive, which differs from the magisterial in its freer use of illustration, analogy, history, and precedent; and the *tonsorial,* which is merely a clutter of quotations from other opinions.

Cardozo offers examples of each category by quoting other judges, but he would have done as well to limit the illustrations to his own opinions, as I shall now try to do.

Here is a good example of his magisterial style. A pacifist attacked the validity of a California statute that required all students in a state university to take a course in military science and tactics. The Supreme Court rejected the argument, and Cardozo made this statement in a concurring opinion:

Never in our history has the notion been accepted, or even, it is believed, advanced, that acts thus indirectly related to service in the camp or field are so tied to the practice of religion as to be exempt, in laws or in morals, from regulation by the state . . . The right of private judgment has never yet been so exalted above the powers and the compulsion of the agencies of government. One who is a martyr to a principle . . . does not prove by his martyrdom that he has kept within the law. (*Hamilton* v. *Regents of the University of California*, 293 U.S. 245)

The laconic and conversational styles are often laced with maxims to illuminate the point to be made. Cardozo admired Holmes intensely for his brevity and pungency, and on this occasion emulated him almost to the point of imitation:

Liberty of contract is not an absolute concept. It is relative to many conditions of time and place and circumstance. The Constitution has not ordained that the forms of business shall be cast in imperishable moulds.

A literary allusion can be used to give point and emphasis to statements otherwise almost too plain:

Aviation is today an established method of transportation. The future, even the near future will make it still more general. The city that is without the foresight to build the ports for the new traffic may soon be left behind in the race for competition. Chalcedon was called the city of the blind because its founders rejected the nobler site of Byzantium lying at their feet.

Humor may be allowed to lighten the conversational style, or presumably any style save the magisterial, but, as Cardozo warns, it is chancy. He himself, as chief judge of New York, used it with good effect in a case brought by a plaintiff who had fractured his kneecap riding on a moving belt in Coney Island called "The Flopper." Cardozo, denying him relief on the eminently sensible ground that one who takes part in such a sport accepts the dangers that inhere in it insofar as they are obvious, commented:

The antics of the clown are not the paces of the cloistered cleric. The rough and boisterous joke, the horseplay of the crowd, evokes its own guffaws, but they are not the pleasures of tranquility. The plaintiff was not seeking a retreat for meditation. Visitors were tumbling about the belt to the merriment of onlookers when he made his choice to join them. He took the chance of a like fate with whatever damage to his body might ensue from such a fall. The timorous may stay at home. (*Murphy v. Steeplechase Amusement Co.,* 250 N.Y. 479)

But the demonstrative or persuasive is Cardozo's most characteristic style. Rarely was he sure enough to use the magisterial, and his more difficult cases were beyond the laconic. Here we see him wrestling with the agonizing question of whether or not a man, sentenced by a trial court to life imprisonment for murder in the second degree, may be executed when the state, appealing his conviction, has obtained the death sentence in a second trial resulting in a verdict of murder in the first. Cardozo, writing for the majority of the

Supreme Court, held that the defendant had not been placed in double jeopardy and must die:

The state is not attempting to wear the accused out by a multitude of cases with accumulated trials. It asks no more than this, that the case against him shall go on until there shall be a trial free from the corrosion of substantial legal error. (*Palko* v. *State of Connecticut,* 58 Sup. Ct. Rep. 149)

There is here no organ note of judgment from the sky to blast the unhappy defendant. Division among the cases is readily admitted, even that the line of division, in a hasty survey, may seem "wavering and broken." Proper analysis, however, will induce a different view. Then will emerge "the perception of a rationalizing principle which gives the discrete instances a proper order and coherence."

But the defendant must not die for subtleties. The reason must be clear, and Cardozo attempts to persuade us that it is:

On which side of the line the case made out by the appellant has appropriate location must be the next inquiry and the final one. Is that kind of double jeopardy to which the statute has subjected him a hardship so acute and shocking that our polity will not endure it? Does it violate those "fundamental principles of liberty and justice which lie at the base of all our civil and political institutions"? The answer must surely be "no."

One may regret that Cardozo went on to conclude his opinion with the dictum that the second trial was not only no cruelty to the defendant but not even "vexation in any immoderate degree"! The wretched man will die, it almost seems, for the perfect balance of the law. The privilege of appeal, granted to the state by the statute in question, is no "seismic innovation":

The edifice of justice stands, its symmetry, to many, greater than before.

Another example of the careful balancing of opposing precedents and the arrival at a conclusion almost in the manner of a brief is Cardozo's opinion for the New York Court of Appeals supporting its holding to admit evidence against a defendant to a larceny charge despite the fact that this evidence has been obtained in a police search made without a warrant. "Shall the criminal go free because the constable has blundered?" Cardozo, replying to his own question in the negative, supports his position more like an advocate than a judge:

We are confirmed in this conclusion when we reflect how far-reaching in its effect upon society the new consequences would be. The pettiest peace officer would have it in his power, through overzeal or indiscretion, to confer immunity upon an offender for crimes the most flagitious. A room is searched against the law, and the body of a murdered man is found. If the place of discovery may not be proved, the other circumstances may be insufficient to connect the defendant with the crime . . . Like instances can be multiplied. We may not subject society to these dangers until the Legislature has spoken with a clearer voice . . . The question is whether protection for the individual would not be gained at a disproportionate loss of protection for society. On the one side is the social need that crime shall be repressed. On the other, the social need that law shall not be flouted by the insolence of office. There are dangers in any choice. (*People* v. *Defoe*, 242 N.Y. 13)

Examples of the refined style may be found anywhere in Cardozo, for his thinking is always subtle and deep. I take almost at random a passage from *Babington* v. *Yellow Taxi Corporation*, 250 N.Y. 14, which decided that a cab driver, killed in a collision after a police officer had jumped on his running board and ordered him to pursue a fleeing criminal, had died while in the performance of his duties for his employer. Cardozo cited an English statute of 1285:

The horse has yielded to the motor car as an instrument of pursuit and flight. The ancient ordinance abides as an interpreter of present duty. Still, as in the days of Edward I, the citizenry may be called upon to enforce the justice of the state, not faintly and with lagging steps, but honestly and bravely and with whatever implements and facilities are convenient and at hand. The incorporeal being, the Yellow Taxi Corporation, would have been bound to respond in that spirit to the summons of the officer if it had been sitting in the driver's seat.

Cardozo concludes his essay on law and literature by affirming that, although a judge or advocate is expounding a science, yet is he still in the process of exposition, practicing an art. The muses may look at him "a bit impatiently," but if the work is finally done they will yet "take him by the hand." I have no doubt that they have clasped Cardozo to their heart.

The Roman Empire
of Pierre Corneille

VOLTAIRE WAS troubled by the tragedies of Corneille, which he edited, because the characters so frequently fall short of neoclassical standards of noble conduct. They have mixed motives: their sexual desire is tangled with ambition, their ambition with jealousy, their jealousy with vindictiveness. The women spit hate at each other; the men are childish in their boasting. One mother asks her son to kill his fiancée; another begs her lover to kill her son. One Roman governor threatens a Christian virgin with prostitution; another sends his son-in-law to the block by perversely misinterpreting a plea for mercy from a general whose favor he covets. Voltaire suggested that some of these situations smack more of the comic than the tragic, but today we no longer care much about this distinction. What begins to be important to us is that these strange, clumsy, often naive characters take on, with deeper acquaintance, a distinct relation to our own era — the era that was born in 1914.

It was less so in the early works. Corneille was thirty when he wrote *Le Cid,* a swashbuckling drama full of glorious verse with as silly a blow-up of the Gallic concept of military glory or *gloire* as the giddiest French patriot could want. Then his success was turned to ashes by a jealous literary clique which received the support of Cardinal Richelieu, and *Le Cid* was "condemned" by the Institute. This was the tragedian's first brush with absolute power, and he never forgot it. For four years he sulked, but when he wrote his next tragedy, he showed that he had learned his lesson. *Horace* was dedicated to the Cardinal himself in language even more obsequious than what contemporary manners required.

What came out of Corneille's conflict with the mighty prime minister was a permanent sense of the dark path to which *gloire* ineluctably leads. Ever afterward he was to say to his theater audiences in his own rough, blunt way: "All right, I'll go along with you; *gloire* is what we all must worship. But don't fool yourself that it means the rise of European culture through the enlightened example of the most glorious nation, France of today or Rome of yesterday. What it really boils down to is military conquest. Let us face frankly what our most glorious men and women really want: power, pure and simple."

Consider the theme of *Horace*. The rivalry between Rome and Albe, two states of equal power, is to be submitted to arbitration in the form of a duel between two teams of selected warriors. The nation with the winning team will thereafter take political precedence, but it is stipulated that the loser shall suffer neither material deprivation nor spiritual humiliation. The duel is to be viewed in the light of a political coin tossing. Yet everyone in Rome and everyone in Albe at once recognizes that victory is still everything — victory is *gloire*. And the victorious Horace does not hesitate to assassinate his grief-crazed sister when she curses Rome, the winner. Audiences before our era used to be appalled by this. They had not known Nazi Germany.

Corneille was always concerned with the Roman Empire, sometimes in its greatness but more often in its decline, the latter being comparable to the decline of the Anglo-American cultural and military empire of our century before the new barbarians in fascist and communist countries. Of course, Anglo-Saxon heroic ideals, like Roman ones, are still proclaimed, but they are also openly jeered at, and the man who talks about George Washington and his cherry tree will risk seeming as pompous and hypocritical as some old Roman senator in the reign of Caracalla wheezing about Horatius at the bridge. This jeering, however, is often the mask of nostalgia. In Corneille's ancient world, as in our modern one, there is a hankering after lost valor, a subdued yearning for past glory, a frustrated feeling that there should be some way to escape the deepening materialism of the age.

If we consider Corneille's Roman tragedies, not in the order in which they were composed, but in the chronological order of the eras they depict, it is possible to make out a history of the rise and fall of the empire based on the rise and fall of the concept of *gloire*.

Horace, of course, represents the dawn of Roman glory. It has an epic theme; its hero is endowed with a touch of the superman — or of the monster — whichever way one sees it. It is his destiny to establish the faith. By placing the tragedy in a mythical era Corneille was able to avoid many of the doubts and perplexities that attend the examination of moral problems closer to his or our own day. The poem is simple, but it is perfect.

Nicomède brings us into actual Roman history, in Bithynia just after the death of Hannibal in 183 B.C. The Roman republic, with the end of the second Punic War, is already mistress of most of the known world. Her ambassador to King Prusias, Flaminius, is a cold, shrewd diplomat of the brand of Talleyrand. He sides first with one and then another faction of the Bithynian court in his relentless policy of dividing and weakening the powers of Asia Minor so that Roman influence may prevail. To Flaminius the heroic Nicomède, the spoiled Attale, the beautiful, noble-minded Laodice, the weak, crafty Prusias and his unscrupulous queen, are so many pawns to be manipulated in the interests of his government. Roman justice and virtue exist, to be sure, but they are cold and distant. Rome, we learn, has refused to connive in the betrayal of Hannibal, but Flaminius himself, for reasons of personal revenge, has had a hand in it. The state is still grand, but the servants are already flawed. In the ambassador's condescension and self-satisfaction we may recall the demeanor of British officers in India. Rome loses a round in the end of *Nicomède,* but it is obvious to all at the final curtain who is going to win the game.

Gloire now has passed to the Bithynian prince, Nicomède, whose mighty arm has won his ungrateful father three crowns. He is the most attractive hero of all the plays: his boldness, his wit, and his sarcasm are effectively employed in tight situations where the immediate odds seem always against him. He is fearless, generous, and amusing; he dominates the court as much through his personality as through the reputation of his victories. We feel that he represents the high spirit and vivid individuality that the blanket of Roman rule must ultimately smother. If there are to be heroes in the future they will have to be Roman heroes, and we wonder already how many of these there will be.

Sertorius takes us to 72 B.C.; the republic has succumbed to the dictatorship of Sulla. The grand old general for whom the tragedy is named has established a rebellious state in Spain and has called to his standard all those who believe in the old Roman values. But there is already something a bit quaint and old-fashioned about him, as symbolized by his ridiculous passion for the superb Viriate, Queen of Lusitania, and he falls an easy victim to the treachery of his own lieutenant. Sertorius is the Roman republic in its senility; Pompée, the heir of Sulla, represents the coming order.

Pompée, to be sure, is a great man, brilliantly effective in peace and in war, but he is a frank opportunist. He has not only divorced the wife he adored, Aristie, to marry the dictator's daughter; he expects Aristie to understand this and to sympathize with him. Of course, he will repudiate his new consort the moment Sulla is out of power and rewed his true love. Will that not make things all right? Aristie does not see it that way at all. When Pompée naively asks her, given Sulla's absolute power, what else he could have done, she replies simply:

> *"Suivre en tous lieux, seigneur, l'exil de votre femme."*

If virtue has passed in the middle east to such princes as Nicomède, in Rome it seems to have passed to the women. Aristie disdains to be practical, as will her successor Cornelie in *La Mort de Pompée*. But let it be noted that the women opposed to Rome, Viriate and the heroine of *Sophonisbe,* show the same indomitable spirit. This raises the question of whether Corneille considers women really capable of *gloire*. When Sophonisbe boasts that she derives as much satisfaction in taking her lover away from a rival as in gaining his love for herself, and when Viriate says that liberty is nothing when the world is free, that the sight of a neighbor in chains is what gives it its value, is the author not implying that their efforts to be heroic are just a touch infantile? And that a Rome where only women have such aspirations is already decadent?

La Mort de Pompée falls in 48 B.C.; Rome is now under a benevolent despotism. At least Corneille found it benevolent. I have little question that he saw Julius Caesar and Augustus as God's answer to Roman civil discord, as he saw Louis XIV as the deus ex machina of the tragedy of the Fronde. Caesar in *Pompée* is almost superhuman: he moves armies and manipulates peoples; he takes in forests without missing trees; he is magnanimous, just, and a passionate lover. But he is also shrewd and cynical. It is possible to play him as secretly relieved that Ptolemy has got rid of his old enemy, Pompée, and hypocritically making political hay out of the opportunity of denouncing the assassination. In the same way one can interpret Auguste in *Cinna* in the way Napoleon did, as pardoning the conspirators in the end, not from any bigness of heart, but because he has coolly come to the conclusion that the mood of the time calls more for mercy than rigor. A world ruler must be above even the finest emotions, as he must, on occasion, be above ordinary morals. For Caesar the end may justify the means, but only for Caesar. Emperors are almost too great for *gloire;* it is better left for their generals. *Gloire* has become a gesture, even a rather theatrical one, in contrast to the power politics of the Roman Empire.

Yet the departure of *gloire* will still be fatal to the empire. The politics will not be enough. In *Othon* we are thrown into the murky world of the later Caesars. It is 69 A.D., the year of the three emperors, the year that followed the assassination of Nero, and the last day of the six months' reign of Galba. The "hero" is a sorry contrast to Horace. Othon has been a favorite of Nero's, to whom he has surrendered his wife. In Galba's court he is a desperate man, proposing marriage first to the daughter of an imperial favorite, then to the emperor's niece, sharing with each of them the knowledge that only by becoming emperor can he hope to save himself and probably them from assassination. He is distinguishable from the more frankly opportunistic Vinius only when he spurns the latter's suggestion that, once emperor, he may divorce the woman to whom he owes his crown. This is a rather attenuated virtue. It is hard to imagine Horace boasting about it.

Attila is the last chapter of imperial history; it offers some chilling parallels. The moral degradation of Europe under the Hitlerian terror is seen in the paralysis of Rome and her allies. The hostage kings of the Ostrogoths and the Gepidi stand about, helpless ornaments, in the court of the Hun conqueror, their courage turned to shrillness, their ingenuity to idle boasts, like the Grand Duke Vladimir, whom the Fuehrer would have made czar of the Ukraine. The only Roman in the play, Princess Honorie, loses her last shred of dignity in her attempt to marry the dictator, for the sake of her country, while hanging on to her old love, and then rejecting Attila, her patriotism forgotten, because she discovers his passion for Ildione. Honorie's *gloire* has sunk to vanity; her nobility is shrill. Rome matters less to her than her own self-esteem. She is willing to die, yes, but to satisfy her pique.

Only the miracle of Attila's massive hemorrhage can save them all; only the flood of his own blood can prevent the bloodbath of Europe. But even this is illusory. The audience of *Attila,* like that of *Othon,* knew that the good news at the final curtain would prove only a temporary respite to general disaster.

Must our civilization end as Rome ended? Is there any alternative to the pursuit of *gloire* followed by the loss of *gloire?* What about Christianity? Corneille devotes two of the Roman plays to martyrs, *Polyeucte* and *Théodore,* but the solution of faith and grace seems to be one offered to individuals rather than nations. The latter must go the way of Rome, and the future of France in the glory of Louis XIV is explicitly predicted in *Attila*. But if the Sun King will be the Augustus of a Gallic empire, who will be its Hun conqueror?

Attila himself might be any dictator today, communist or fascist. His idea of *gloire* is to conquer and rule as much of the world as possible. He scorns what he considers the trumpery values of decadent cultures; he orders captive monarchs about like valets. To lie, to cheat, to torture, to kill, all are permissible to attain world rule. And the rule itself is everything; its attainment, which to Horace was life itself, is nothing. To win by wile is better than to win by battle. As Octar says of his chief:

> *Il aime à conquérir, mais il haït les batailles;*
> *Il veut que son nom seul renverse les murailles;*
> *Et plus grand politique encore que grand guerrier,*
> *Il tient que les combats sentent l'aventurier.*

Is that the end of every culture: a barbarian, with loyal aides? At least we escaped Nixon. Perhaps the darkling plain and the ignorant, clashing armies may be avoided as well. Yet I have always felt at home in Corneille's great chronicle of the ancient world. Does not *Othon* evoke the hell of a political scene in Moscow where there is no dignity, no integrity, no safety outside of each man's capacity to forecast the political future? In *Tite et Berenice* what do we have but the pathos of the Duke of Windsor? In *Cinna* what but the conspiracy against de Gaulle by the African imperialists? I can adjust my view of the confrontation between Viriate and Aristie in *Sertorius* to one between two lacquered dragons of Manhattan cosmetics, an Elizabeth Arden and a

Helena Rubinstein, and Viriate's proposal to the old general reminds me of a president's widow offering her hand to a Greek shipper. And what American son and husband does not recognize the heroine of *Rodogune* when she offers *her* hand to that one of two brothers who will bring her his mother's head?

Racine's world is full of men and women who give up all for love: Phèdre, Roxane, Pyrrhus, Hermione. No doubt this is a reason for his greater popularity. But how many such heroines or heroes do we meet in daily twentieth-century life? Corneille shows us his lovers as balancing the rewards of the world against the rewards of passion and the nobility of power against the nobility of love. The Carthaginian heroine of *Sophonisbe,* who repudiates one husband when he becomes a prisoner of war, marries another to carry on the battle, and finally swallows poison to avoid being led in triumph through Rome, can still boast that the greatest pleasure of her life has been in stealing a lover from a rival. The noble Pompée, in *Sertorius,* demands that his wife submit to the humiliation of divorce so that he may marry the daughter of the dictator, Sulla, fully intending to repudiate the latter after Sulla's anticipated demise. And the Eastern empress in *Pulcherie* solves her problem of choosing an imperial consort who will not dominate her politically by selecting a general who has loved her for a decade on condition that the marriage be not consummated. What made Corneille's characters grotesque to Voltaire is precisely what makes them real today; they are always trying to have their cake and eat it. They want the power *and* the glory, and in the long run this is not possible. They are greedy, but they are true.

Jane Austen and the Good Life

JANE AUSTEN HAS always had to put up with a certain amount of condescension, even from her admirers. It used to be the fashion to illustrate her books as if they were juveniles, with pictures of dainty ladies on tiny feet and in huge hats tripping down cobbled streets to shop or make calls. And who is not tired of having it pointed out that she wrote six novels during the Napoleonic wars without ever mentioning Napoleon's name? I was delighted recently to discover that she had spoken of this herself, and as a fault, but not with a grovelling twentieth-century guilt at having scanted her duty to history. She simply regretted that she had not used the emperor to provide her with an artistic contrast. She considered that *Pride and Prejudice* was "too light and bright and sparkling" and needed "the history of Buonaparte to increase the reader's delight at the playfulness and epigrammaticism of the general style." She would have shaped Buonaparte for her fictional purposes as Tolstoy was to do in *War and Peace*.

The great events of the world do not much help the novelist of any age in his task. As Mary McCarthy has pointed out, the world of the novel is essentially a reasonable one, and the mighty things, at least of our time — genocide, the bomb, the population explosion — are essentially unreason-able. Jane Austen was just as aware of Napoleon as we are aware of Moscow and Peking (more so, perhaps, with a favorite brother on active duty in the navy and a first cousin married to a Frenchman guillotined in the terror), but he was not useable. She rejected him, as she rejected the Prince Regent's librarian's suggestion that she do a book on the House of Coburg, in order to pursue the task that Charlotte Brontë and George Eliot were also to set for themselves: that of finding the good life.

Every time that I reread Jane Austen's peerless six, I dis-cover that, although I always rate them closely together, I find that the order of my preference changes. In youth *Emma* and *Pride and Prejudice* were my favorites. In middle age they are *Sense and Sensibility* and *Mansfield Park,* and, after them, *Persuasion.* To me these three are bathed in a mood of what, for lack of a better term, I shall call moral beauty. The long, grave struggles of Marianne Dashwood, of Fanny Price, and of Anne Elliot for a life that is worth the living seem to me the finest parts of Jane Austen's work.

In *Emma* the heroine's path to happiness is essentially smooth. She has only to wake up to what is there before her. And Elizabeth Bennet and Darcy in *Pride and Prejudice* are kept apart by a series of simple misunderstandings on Eliza-beth's part. Darcy's pride, once comprehended, is no hin-drance. Indeed, it is an integral part of his sex appeal. But Marianne Dashwood in *Sense and Sensibility* is brought close to death by her reckless passion for Willoughby, and Fanny Price in *Mansfield Park* must endure a youth of mortification and semi-servitude before Edmund Bertram learns to value the love that he has inspired. For Marianne and for Fanny the search for the good life requires patience, courage, and discipline.

What, then, is this "good life" for a Jane Austen heroine? Well, to begin with, it is limited to a very small part of the social structure. The top of society has been made a desert by the arrogance and worldliness of such rich or titled folk as Mrs. Ferrars, Lady Catherine de Bourgh, and Sir Walter Elliot. Only Elizabeth Bennet, cleverest of the heroines, can find her oasis there. And if one descends the social ladder too far, to the Price family, for example, in *Mansfield Park,* one finds that Jane Austen was clearly of the opinion that the good life was not compatible with noisy, undisciplined children let loose in small rooms. No, there should be some degree of affluence to provide space, both for solitude and for genteel gatherings, in houses that should be always elegant, even when simple, and should, if the countryside permits, look out on pleasant landscapes. Jane Austen lived in an era of such universal good taste (almost inconceivable to us) that it was inevitable for her and her contemporaries to associate outward order with inward serenity.

Also in the good life there should be time for reading, music, drawing, and for edifying conversation. And in the good marriage there should be compatibility as well as love, and money as well as mutual respect, although, as Catherine Morland points out in *Northanger Abbey,* it does not matter which spouse supplies the money. But above all, both in life and marriage, there should be a guiding philosophy to restrain the individual from excess, the excess of hoping too much or of despairing too much, and a constant resignation to the whims of providence that may at any moment dash the cup from even devoutly worshiping lips. This last is most important of all.

Now if one is going to take the attitude, because today any young man should be able to support himself and because class distinctions have largely dwindled to eccentricities, that

Jane Austen was a snob to premise marriage on a bank account and some degree of compatibility of social background, one may as well shut up her novels. She was of her time, and she accepted her time, not as an ideal one but as something to be made the best of. In her day (and indeed in all days but our own) it was a very dangerous thing to run out of money, and only a fool ignored this. But this did not mean that money was to be coveted unduly. When Elizabeth Bennet argues that, if it be imprudent for Wickham to court a portionless girl, it must be wise for him to court a rich one, Jane Austen makes it very plain that her heroine is joking. Such conduct on Wickham's part would be "mercenary," and to be mercenary is being bad indeed. Simply because a line is hard to draw, does not excuse a man from drawing it.

Some of Jane Austen's own contemporaries had a bit of trouble with this line. It bothered Sir Walter Scott, for example, that Elizabeth's heart should soften toward Darcy as she contemplates his handsome park at Pemberley. But I imagine that Jane Austen would have replied that so long as her heroine was not primarily motivated by the park, it was a perfectly proper item on the list of Darcy's attractions. Pemberley is part of Darcy's sex appeal, as Donwell Abbey is part of Knightley's, as social position is part of Emma Woodhouse's and as poverty and loneliness are part of Fanny Price's. No doubt it is nobler in mating to be drawn only to the person of one's partner, and those who are able so neatly to compartmentalize their feelings are quite right to scold Jane Austen.

Money, then, must receive its rightful due, but not a jot more than its rightful due. This is also true of the separation of classes. Jane Austen finds it manifestly absurd for Lady Catherine de Bourgh to consider Elizabeth Bennet unworthy of her nephew, but she also finds it very wrong of Emma

Woodhouse to persuade the illegitimate, nameless Harriet Smith that she is a fit match for Mr. Elton. Elizabeth will grace Pemberley; Harriet is not up to a rectory. That is the eighteenth century, and that is Jane Austen. But the good life could still be attained even by a poor girl, within the hierarchies of that harshly divided world. This is the theme of *Mansfield Park*.

Fanny Price is surely the least loved of Jane Austen's heroines, but she had grown on me steadily through the years. She is not gay like Elizabeth Bennet or pert like Emma; she lacks Catherine Morland's ingenuousness and Anne Elliot's charm, but then she is poorer and lower born than any of them. She comes alone as a child to the hostile luxury of Mansfield Park, a waif suddenly confronted with the splendor of a rich baronet's household, and she must put together her life out of the scraps that are flung to her. Only by rejecting the bad things that she sees — the snobbishness, the greediness, the sensuality, the flippancy, the hardness — and grasping to her heart the good — the love of graceful dimensions, the opportunity of libraries, the approaches to God and serenity in quiet and solitude — can she come out on top.

She has no help from anyone, except a few kind words from Edmund. Her other cousins make fun of her. Her uncle, Sir Thomas, is grave and terrifying, and he will not care for the inclinations of the heart when it comes to an advantageous match for a poor niece. Aunt Bertram is indolent, Aunt Norris tyrannical. The first regards Fanny as a paid companion, the second as a serving maid. A young neighbor, Henry Crawford, is out to break her heart, perhaps to seduce her. And to add to her woes, she is in love with Edmund, who doesn't even know it. But Fanny will never take second best: of that she is always sure. She will wait for

Edmund, though she knows her love to be impossible, for even if by a miracle he should ever want to marry her, he could not do so without his family's consent. Yes, that is another of the tough conditions in Jane Austen's world. Even an unreasonable parent's consent must be obtained, even the horrible General Tilney's in *Northanger Abbey*.

Fanny must be the rebuttal to those who claim that Jane Austen is basically worldly. She stands out against everybody who urges compromise. She has no one to advise her or help her in her crisis. In the household of her rich uncle, Sir Thomas Bertram, she is a kind of upper servant. She is penniless and without prospects. Yet a rich and attractive young man, Henry Crawford, suddenly offers her his hand and fortune, and everyone, including her beloved cousin Edmund, congratulates her on her good luck. But she turns him down. Cinderella rejects Prince Charming! Why? Because she is in love with Edmund? But his heart is elsewhere engaged. No, the real reason is that she has seen Crawford heartlessly flirting with *both* her cousins, Maria and Julia, one of whom is engaged to another man. She knows he is rotten.

Crawford is nonetheless sincerely in love. His character is even improved by the experience, as Fanny recognizes. He goes up to London to obtain a commission for her brother, earning a valid claim to her gratitude. Furthermore, her rejection of him must be attended by disagreeable consequences to herself. Her uncle will accuse her of wilfulness, self-conceit, and ingratitude and send her off to her parents' humble home in Portsmouth, that she may have a taste of the poverty from which he has rescued her and to which she can always be returned if she persists in rejecting eligible suitors. So what will poor Fanny have gained?

Simply her soul. Henry Crawford and his sister, Mary, for all their charm and popularity, are deeply corrupted individuals. And Fanny has divined this with much less information than the reader has. *She* has not heard them discussing Henry's cold-blooded plan to amuse himself for a few weeks by making Fanny fall in love with him — a plan which of course backfires. But Fanny has observed how Henry has behaved during the rehearsal of *Lovers' Vows,* the play that the young people of Mansfield are putting on for the neighboring gentry. She has watched him undermining Maria's engagement. His conduct has been clearly incompatible with the good life.

Much has been written about Jane Austen's prudishness about the amateur theatricals at Mansfield. Why should the Bertrams and Crawfords not put on a play? But *Lovers' Vows* to Sir Thomas Bertram must have seemed like *Hair* to a Westchester banker in 1968. Could ladies, unmarried ladies, appear in it? With its frank love scenes and its suggestiveness, it represents the intrusion of the worst of London into the sanctity of Mansfield Park. It is loud; it is vulgar; it is intimate. It is the bad life.

Fanny alone of all the household has nothing directly to do with it. She will not take a part. She is absolutely firm, as she will be later in her refusal to accept Crawford. Fanny may be a trifle fastidious about the noise and sloppy habits of her own family in Portsmouth, but there is never any danger that she will compromise her moral standards to get away from them. She is strong because her inner life accords with her outward decorum. Contrast her with Mary Crawford:

"I shall soon be rested," said Fanny; "to sit in the shade on a fine day and look upon verdure, is the most perfect refreshment."
    After sitting a while, Miss Crawford was up again. "I must leave," said she; "resting fatigues me. — I have looked across the ha-ha till I am weary."

What we see in the Crawfords and in the Bertram sisters is outward decorum over a flawed interior. This will never do. Here is how Jane Austen sees Julia Bertram:

The politeness which she had been brought up to practise as a duty, made it impossible for her to escape; while the want of that higher species of self-command, that just consideration of others, that knowledge of her own heart, that principle of right which had not formed any essential part of her education, made her miserable under it.

It is all very well to call Fanny and Edmund prigs, but they are ranged against adversaries so dangerous that even priggishness may not be a weapon that they can afford to discard. Henry Crawford has made both the Bertram girls miserable; he will ultimately destroy Maria's marriage and reputation, and he has entertained a project that might have resulted in Fanny's seduction. Through all Jane Austen's veils we catch a glimpse of Lovelace. And his sister has plotted nothing less than the undermining of Edmund's chosen career; she yearns to turn a minister into a social idler. There is wickedness in *Mansfield Park;* under the good manners, the quiet routine, the gentle chat, there is a note of Miltonic struggle. In the end Jane Austen ceases to laugh at Mrs. Norris; we learn that Sir Thomas himself has come to feel her "as an hourly evil":

She was regretted by no one at Mansfield. She had never been able to attach even those she loved best, and since Mrs. Rushworth's elopement, her temper had been in a state of such irritation, as to make her everywhere tormenting. Not even Fanny had tears for Aunt Norris — not even when she was gone forever.

In the fullness of time the patient and intrepid Fanny comes into her own. Edmund is at last cured of his infatuation for Mary Crawford and comes to see that Fanny will be the perfect parson's wife, and Fanny herself is finally justified in making use of evidence in her possession to prove to him that Mary is "mercenary." Even a good girl, after all, must occasionally use her claws in the jungle. But never too much, never in excess. Fanny wins her Edmund in the end, together with the love and respect of all the Bertrams, but she is always aware that it could have worked out very differently and that she might just as easily have spent the rest of her life sitting on the sofa in the drawing room reading aloud to Aunt Bertram. Fanny has accepted the universe.

Fanny has had too hard a lot to develop much charm, but not so Anne Elliot in *Persuasion,* who is as attractive as she is good. She has been argued out of an engagement to a young naval officer seven years before the action of the novel commences, by her mentor, Lady Russell. Anne has not done wrong, according to her creator, in bowing to Lady Russell. Her fault, such as it is, lies simply in her failure to have tried harder to talk Lady Russell out of it. The sanctity of the older generation is strictly preserved in Jane Austen, but no more than it is in Trollope or Thackeray. Life, however, brings Anne a glorious second chance with her sailor, and, unlike most beneficiaries of such chances, she grabs it! But in the ecstasy of this long-awaited engagement she must not and does not lose her head. She will not risk all by violence as Marianne Dashwood did:

An interval of meditation, serious and grateful, was the best corrective of everything dangerous in such high-wrought felicity, and she went to her room and grew steadfast and fearless in the thankfulness of her enjoyment.

To get money or social position or just a man — there is no great trick to that. Jane Austen tosses cheap successes to her cheap characters. A true sophisticate, she knew how easily the "great World" is duped. The mean and vulgar Lucy Steele can insinuate herself into the affections of Robert Ferrars and of his ultrasnobbish mother; the unscrupulous Willoughby can marry a fortune, and the cheat Wickham can be established by the man he tried to ruin; it is even prognosticated in the end of *Persuasion* that Mrs. Clay may end up as Lady Elliot. But what have such trashy folk to do with the good life? The finest taste is kept for the finest wine. Charlotte Lucas in *Pride and Prejudice* does not do absolutely wrong to marry the absurd Mr. Collins, but she would do better to become a governess. Fanny Price would never have so compromised.

Two Conversation Pieces:
The Astors and the Vanderbilts

THE ASTORS AND the Vanderbilts occupy the curious chapter, halfway between fact and fantasy, in American history that is allotted to "society" people in our literature. If you want to read about how their fortunes were made, you will find a good deal of dry but solid material, but if you want to know how it was spent, you will find yourself staring at a shelf of glossy texts by hack writers whose only research has been in the society columns of old newspapers. No serious historian has touched the subject, nor will any, until the Astors and Vanderbilts have acquired the dignifying varnish of time. It is perfectly respectable in academic circles to pry into the smallest bit of gossip about the Medici, or the court at Byzantium, but Fifth Avenue and Newport are forbidden territory.

Perhaps historians are wise. Reading the junk about Commodore Vanderbilt and his descendants, one wonders if some of it will not stick to anyone who ventures into the field. The silly books all tell the same story in the same way. There is the tough, swearing old Commodore and his public-be-damning son, William Henry; there is Alva and her costume ball and how she tricked Mrs. Astor into calling on her; there is the forced marriage of Consuelo to the Duke of Marlborough; there is a glance at Alfred going down on the *Lusitania,* a good deal about little Gloria and the battle over her custody, and then a burst of prose about Grace Vanderbilt and Mrs. Twombly at the opera, all to a twitter of terms such as *dowager, grande dame, château, châtelaine, formidable, impeccable,* or *exclusive,* and to a huge heap of bad photographs that dwindles, on closer examination, into a small one, for the repetitions seem endless. One can learn much more about the clan by a study of a conversation piece by Seymour J. Guy, which hangs in "Biltmore."

We should first, however, put forth the query: what is a family, or even more simply, what is a Vanderbilt? The Commodore had thirteen children; his son William Henry had eight. The descendants of these two, living and dead, amount to a total of well over four hundred souls. Those who bear (or bore) the patronym *Vanderbilt* are but a tiny fraction of this total and do not, at least today, even include the richest of them. The issue of William Henry at the present time numbers many individuals who owe their fortunes to blood strains other than his: Whitneys, Burdens, Twomblys, Bostwicks, Webbs, Millikens, Osborns. What has a social historian accomplished by limiting himself to those members who bore the patronym? Which, for example, was the more representative great-grandson of William Henry: Cornelius Vanderbilt IV, the seven-times-married journalist of only modest means, or William A. M. Burden, the multimillionaire investment banker who, incidentally, bears a distinct resemblance to their common ancestor?

And yet, when this has been pointed out, there still remains — or at least remained — a Vanderbilt family with a

style, a flair, a verve, very much their own. Certainly, at one
point, they looked alike. Perhaps the fact that the Commodore married his first cousin contributed to this. And they
were handsome, too. The Guy conversation piece shows William Henry and his wife, Maria, with their eight children,
three in-laws and two devoted servants (the latter just visible,
peeping over the shoulders of the others in the back of the
painting) . The year is 1873, and the terrible old Commodore
is still alive and holding on to the fortune with a very firm
grasp. Nobody even can be sure that 99 percent of it will be
left (as it was) to William Henry rather than to the many
others. The latter's family are gathered together in the comfortable and luxurious, but essentially still modest bourgeois
interior of his big brownstone house on Fifth Avenue and
42nd Street, opposite to where the public library now stands.
The pictures that clutter the walls, in elaborate gilt frames,
show the beginnings of his undistinguished collection of
nineteenth-century academic landscapes and "story" pictures.
William Henry is comfortably seated by the fire, a plain,
good, prosperous burgher of few visible pretensions, proud
of his bad pictures and of his large family. Maria, seated
placidly by his side in sober black, accepting his wealth
without dazzlement, seems the epitome of the good burgher's
wife. But the story is just beginning. One can see it in the
children.

It is immediately evident that they outshine their parents
not only in physical appearance, but in dress and deport-
ment. One imagines that they already have a vision of interiors more suited to their elegance and beauty. Margaret
Shepard, the oldest daughter, in sweeping blue, regally
dominates the center of the picture as if to live up to the high
standards of her worldly husband, Elliott Shepard, who sur-

veys her critically. One can almost foresee that he will run
through most of her fortune. Emily Sloane, young bride of
the handsome rug merchant who is buttoning her glove, is
splendid in white silk. Florence and Willie K., both still unmarried, handsomest of all, look as if they were waiting for
the old folks to go to bed so that they could go "on." Young
George, in the center, might be daydreaming of the biggest
palace of all that *he* was one day to build, and Lila, sitting
under the gentle hand of her oldest sister, seems a little princess. And they not only look handsome, they look amiable.
Who could blame even amiable young people for dreams of
grandeur? What else in such an era, with the vision of such
a fortune before them, would we expect them to have? They
might be characters in the opening chapter of a novel by
William Dean Howells. Only one would like to leave them
in that first chapter. One hesitates to turn the page and aban-
don so pleasant a scene.

The Commodore, as I have said, was still alive, alive and
detested. He was never a man to inspire love, and his rough
manners and swearing must have been intensely distasteful
to grown-up granddaughters who wished to conform to the
primmer atmosphere of their day. Commodore Vanderbilt
had been born in the previous century, and he was much
more characteristic of it than he was of the nineteenth. He
belongs to the novels of Smollett, not to those of Thackeray.
As the surviving letters of the generation of Vanderbilts that
preceded him in Staten Island show a greater finish in style
than one would anticipate from the legends of the Commodore's crude language, I suspect that he adopted a rougher
air than had been his birthright for the pleasure of shocking
people, particularly members of his own family. I see him as
one of those individualists who glory in attributing their suc-

cess entirely to their own genius — with no credit to fore-bears. The Commodore, like Napoleon, wanted only to be an ancestor. It must have given them a fierce gratification to see people fawn before him and accept an uncouthness at which, in anybody less rich and powerful, they would have openly sneered. The Commodore, when all is said and done, had a bit of greatness to him, which could not be said of any of his business competitors. But his grandchildren must have been glad to see the old pirate dead and buried and the money safely in their own hands. They had no desire to defy the world. They were friendly folk who liked to be liked.

The style of living of which these young Vanderbilts were dreaming is perfectly illustrated by another conversation piece, of the family of William Astor, painted by Lucius Rossi in the same decade. The Astors in 1878 had no grand-paternal wills to wait for. Unlike the Vanderbilts, they were already at the apex of the social pyramid. There is nothing bourgeois about the ballroom in which they are having tea in the same obviously empty teacups that we see today on the social page in the hands of ladies planning theater bene-fits. The interior is awesomely aristocratic and entirely Eu-ropean; it might be the salon of a great palazzo in Rome or of an old *hôtel* in the Faubourg St. Germain. Between gilded Corinthian columns hangs the sixteenth-century portrait of some ruffed, royal personage. The vaulted ceiling is painted with allegorical pictures. The ladies, doll-like in Worth dresses with fashionably tiny feet resting on cushions, recline on splendid Louis XV chairs. The only American note in the scene is that of the husband, bored and out of it all, holding his newspaper in his hand as if clutching to the only thing in the room for which he has any affinity, totally at odds with his extravagant womenfolk, sharing in none of their pleasures or aspirations, and missing even the heady arrogance of the self-made man who can regard the jewels that cover his wife as emblems of his own masculinity. William Henry Vanderbilt, still bourgeois, is still happy; William Astor, the converted aristocrat, is not. Only women could really enjoy the New York social life of the eighties and nineties.

Commodore Vanderbilt died in 1877 and William H. less than a decade later, so that the eight Vanderbilt children of Guy's painting came into possession (though not in equal shares) of the greatest fortune in the world while they were still young. Their bourgeois era was now over, and they proceeded to build like lords. There were no lights under any of their bushels. The very poorest of the sons, George, was able to build the greatest palace of all: "Biltmore" in Asheville, North Carolina. But the seven others did almost as well. In Newport, in Hyde Park, in Lenox, in Scarborough, in Shelbourne, in Madison, on Long Island, they reared their immense edifices. There seemed no end to it. I doubt that any other group of siblings, outide of royal families, has ever been so magnificently housed. Yet they maintained the family solidarity evoked by the Guy conversation piece. They were always visiting each other, back and forth, helping to fill up the endless guest rooms and the big vellum pages of the leather bound guest books on which they inscribed their pleasant compliments and funny drawings. People could never quite forgive the Vanderbilts for enjoying their money. The rich were supposed to be bored. Hadn't they heard?

Boredom, in time, came, and silliness with it. Perhaps, after all, there is some truth in those "society" books. Look at all those incredible houses in all those incredible pictures. Was it really possible for Alice Vanderbilt to occupy a reproduction of a Loire château right on the Grand Army Plaza for some thirty years, waited on by as many servants, never going into a shop but having shopkeepers come to her, without coming to think of herself, like Mrs. Astor, as a queen? Could her daughter-in-law, Grace, in her eighties, stepping in and out of maroon Rolls-Royces, pretending to shield her face from prying cameras, arriving at the opera, leaving the opera, playing games with delighted reporters, avoid the same delusion? How can one write serious history about people who keep turning themselves into the very figures the hacks write about? Perhaps one can only look nostalgically back to the handsome young people in the Guy conversation piece — before it all happened.

The Astors never really constituted a clan, like the Vanderbilts. The brother of the William shown in the Rossi painting was John Jacob Astor who inherited two thirds of the family fortune and left it to his son, William Waldorf Astor, who moved to England where he purchased a viscountcy from a reluctant crown by his vast public gifts in the First World War. The English Astors have produced many males, but their story belongs to English social history. The only son of the William Astors, John Jacob, seen as a youth in the painting, perished with the *Titanic* and his son, Vincent, the heir of the great bulk of the American fortune, died without issue, leaving it to his widow and to his foundation.

The children of William Astor's daughters — Van Alens, Draytons, Roosevelts, and Wilsons — did not have the clannishness of the Vanderbilts nor did they have the same strong family resemblance. Furthermore, the American male Astors tended to be unsocial, even antisocial. They had a truculent, stiff-necked Germanic quality totally alien to the gregarious and fun-loving Vanderbilts. Thus, whereas the social story of the latter is divided among many, that of the Astors is rep-

resented primarily by one person, Mrs. William Astor. But
she more than made up for this. Her name encompasses her
era. She "incorporated" society and made it big business.

So far as I know, her inner personality — if one existed at
all under the hostess, and there is no assurance that it did —
has been lost. In the conversation piece she is merely regal.
I once spent two hours with one of her grandsons while he
talked about her. Although he had been of college age when
she died and had been devoted to her, every story that he
told me I had already read in one or another of the "society"
books. As the impression of the Parthenon imprinted on a
tourist's eyeball fades with time to be replaced by the post-
card in his album, so has Mrs. Astor's private image been replaced by her public one, even in the minds of her descendants. Perhaps we shall not see her more clearly than in this
glimpse of her in Mrs. Winthrop Chanler's *Roman Spring:*

Mrs. William B. Astor was the acknowledged leader [of New York
society]. She always sat on the right of the host when she went
to dinner parties; she wore a black wig and a great many jewels;
she had pleasant cordial manners and unaffectedly enjoyed her
undisputed position.

Yet there may be some value in viewing her through more
reverent eyes. If the legend is all that is left of her, we may do
well to consider the man who created it. Did Ward Mc-
Allister and Mrs. Astor really organize New York society?
Did he make her queen of it, as Disraeli made Victoria
empress of India? According to his memoirs, it was a perfectly deliberate process:

The first Patriarch Balls were given in the winters of 1872 and
1873. At this period, a great personage (representing a silent
power that had always been recognized and felt in this commu-

nity, so long as I remember, by not only fashionable people, but by the solid old quiet element as well) had daughters to introduce into society, which brought her prominently forward and caused her at once to take a leading position. She possessed great administrative power, and it was soon put to good use and felt by society. I then, for the first time, was brought in contact with this *grande dame,* and at once recognized her ability, and felt that she would become society's leader, and that she was admirably qualified for the position.

Yet even the casual reader of *Society as I Found It* begins to suspect, not simply that the author was a fatuous ass — that is obvious from the first paragraph — but that he must have appeared so even to the world that he thought he was disciplining. One is not surprised to learn that at the end of his life he became a bore and was dropped by society. He had not changed, poor man, but his fashion had. Such is the fate of cotillion leaders.

McAllister, however, recovered some of his reputation, at least to future generations, by writing these memoirs. His case was analogous to that of Marcel Proust's character, the marquise de Villeparisis, whose posthumous autobiography, filled with the great names of her relatives, successfully obscures to posterity the fact that society had shunned her on moral grounds. McAllister has readers today who take entirely for granted that he was once taken as seriously as he claims. But I see him rather as the butt of obscene jokes told over brandy by the very gentlemen whose socially ambitious wives were fluttering over him in the parlor.

McAllisters exist in all ages, in all societies. They are men who are happy to accept eminence in form rather than substance, abandoning the latter to the rougher competitors of their own sex. They are content to settle for the paraphernalia of success: the uniforms, the medals, the sonorous titles, the bobbing and bowing — all the things that emphasize rank and hierarchy. Like sleek, furry squirrels on high perches they can relax their panting hearts as they contemplate large dangerous foes at a safe distance below. One sees McAllisters in those diplomats who adore the seating of dinner parties, in those academicians who love robes and commencement parades, in those military officers who cling to promotion by precedence. As they grow older they begin to lose the awareness that everyone does not share their values. McAllister implies in his memoirs that the neatest trick of his lifetime had been to improvise a ten-day house party of a dozen guests in a deserted country mansion in New Jersey, with only a week's notice in which to arrange for chef, servants, menus, orchestra, food, wine, and horses. "This country party," he baldly states, "I gave in November, 1862." Surely some of his readers, even as late as 1890, his year of publication, must have recalled a campaign waged less successfully in that same November: Burnside's push into Virginia which stalled at Fredericksburg.

The persons whom McAllisters naturally attract and to whom they are naturally attracted are rich, elderly women of fashionable inclinations. There is never any question of sex between the two. If the McAllister is not overtly homosexual, he is at least inclined to be epicene. McAllister himself in his memoirs made much of his gallantry with the "fair sex," but he seemed to feel that this had to be pointed up. His relationship with Mrs. Astor might be described by the biological term: symbiosis. Each benefited from the other. He indulged her fantasy that she was a sultana; she his that he was a grand vizier. They acted out their comedy to the delight of society, whose delight, I suggest, was the point of the whole thing. Mrs. Astor was not crowned by Ward McAllister but by a fancy-dress-party world that wanted a queen. Had she not accepted the role, it would have been offered to another. Somebody had to justify the building of a thousand European châteaux! Rossi painted the dream of American society and through its dream we can know it.

The Late Jamesing of
Early James

E VER SINCE THE appearance of the Scribner edition of
the fiction of Henry James in 1907, there has been a
lively controversy as to whether or not he improved or dam-
aged his work by the extensive revisions he undertook for
this publication. The controversy centers around the earlier
novels, as the later ones, presumably, were already couched
in a style more or less satisfactory to the reviser. *The American,* first published thirty years before in 1877, is reputed to
be the work that received the most extensive re-editing.

Now, thanks to the Scolar Press, we can study a facsimile
reproduction of the galleys of *The American* (taken from
the Macmillan edition of 1883) in which James inserted his
changes. It is thus possible, although difficult, to follow his
correcting process through the multitudinous autograph
marginal additions and typescript insertions. Unfortunately,
James's deletions are usually inked in so heavily that it is
still necessary to go back to a clear copy of the earlier text
to follow his process with any thoroughness. It seems a pity
that there should not have been some method of printing the

deleted material in the Scolar Press edition, but let us be
grateful for what we have.

The great delight of this publication is, of course, in comparing the old and new phrases. Here are some random examples of what to me represent the improvements of the revisions: "young women in long aprons, on high stools" for
"young women in irreproachable toilets"; "a blue satin neck-
tie of too light a shade" for "a cerulean cravat"; "a tale of
the western world [which] showed to that bright alien air,
very much as fine desiccated, 'articulated' specimens,
bleached, monstrous, probably unique, show in the high
light of museums of natural history" for "an intensely western story." I prefer the sentence, "The business of mere
money getting showed only in its ugliness, vast and vague
and dark, like a pirate ship with its lights turned inward," to
its predecessor, "The business of money getting appeared
tolerably dry and sterile." And I see Madame de Bellegarde
more clearly in the later description, "She resembled her
daughter as an insect might resemble a flower," than I do in
the earlier, "She resembled her daughter, and yet she was
utterly unlike her."

Finally, I cannot resist citing the happy transition of the
clause "to drag such a train over a polished floor was a felicity
worth any price" to the later one "to carry about such a mass
of ponderable pleasure would surely be one of the highest
uses of freedom." But one could go on with this indefinitely.

On the debit side, I do not see why "tasted tobacco" is
better than "smoked," or why "I never took any lessons"
should be stiffened to "I never required or received any in-
struction." When Newman says "I'm a highly civilized man,"
I like him much more than when he orates "I have the instincts — have them deeply — if I haven't the forms, of a high
old civilization." And when "wash tubs" become "articles of

vulgar household use," I feel that I have moved from *The American* to *The Ambassadors*.

At times the alterations are almost comical. The dying Valentin in 1877 asks Newman simply if he and Claire have quarreled. In 1907 he asks, "Have you unimaginably quarrelled?" And the murdered Urbain de Bellegarde changes his deathbed note from "I'm dying, dying horribly" to "I'm horribly, helplessly, dying." But the real screamer is the revision of the simple statement that Newman was clean shaven to: "He spoke, as to chin and cheek, of the joys of the matutinal steel."

A more significant change is in the dialogue between Newman and Valentin de Bellegarde about Mlle. Nioche, the gist of which is that Valentin promises to keep his hands off the young copyist until Newman should have been convinced that she is a prostitute. In the 1877 version this bargain is put very bluntly and clearly. But in 1907 James had much more to say about Valentin's immorality. To his hero, Newman, this has now become a kind of quaint liberalism, characteristic of the fine old families, almost charming; he is learning not to cavil at European tolerances. Valentin, in turn, seeks "in all delicacy" a "free hand" under circumstances which will not "shock" his friend. The Newman of the *belle époque,* however, claims that what shocks him is precisely the "delicacy" of Valentin's proposition! This seems a long way from the prairies of the West and the battlefields of the Civil War.

But there is a significant improvement in the scene where Newman is presented to that grim old tyrant, Madame de Bellegarde. In the earlier version he simply "shook hands with her." In the latter he "came sufficiently near to the old lady by the fire to take in that she could offer him no handshake — so that he had the air of waiting, and a little like a customer in a shop, to see what she *would* offer." Here the very drama of the novel is successfully encapsulated.

The younger James never made much of physical embracements, but in his later years he tried to add heat to his love scenes. I have never thought much of the famous clinch between the Prince and Charlotte in *The Golden Bowl*. It embarrasses me faintly, as does the following embellishment of Newman's relations with Claire:

He almost groaned for deep insistence, and he laid his two hands on her with a persuasion that she rose to meet. He let her feel, as he drew her close and bent his face to her, the fullest force of his imposition which she took from him with a silent surrender that he felt long enough to be complete.

On the other hand I think that the ending of the novel has been improved. In the first version we leave Newman staring down into the grate of the ashes to which the fatal letter of Urbain de Bellegarde has been consumed. In the revised version we see Mrs. Tristram, who has always had a *faible* for Newman, raising his hand gravely to her lips as she murmurs "Poor Claire." This finely expresses not only Mrs. Tristram's feeling for the hero, but her sense of all that Claire has so tragically lost.

One can go on indefinitely giving examples, some very striking and some simply amusing, of the hundreds of revisions to which James subjected his tale, but the only question of any importance is what effect these changes had upon the final product. Is *The American* a better book for them? Is it even a different book?

I am afraid that it boils down to a case of *plus ça change*. There is no essential difference in any of the characters or in any incident of the plot. It is the same story with essentially the same interpretations and the same emphases. Oddly enough, James did not even alter the form of the novel to incorporate his later theories of the limitation of the points of view. *The Golden Bowl* and *The Wings of the Dove* are divided into sections, each of which is centered in the consciousness of a single character. The whole of *The Ambassadors* is centered in the consciousness of Lambert Strether. But in *The American* the reader moves in and out of the minds of different characters in the same chapter. I suppose that even an author as industrious as James quailed before the task of changing this.

If, then, *The American* of 1907 is essentially the same book that it was in 1877, what is the effect of the revisions? Do they improve or damage the original version? Is this a matter of simply adding up the revisions that are improvements and comparing them with the total of those that may be considered damaging? It seems to me that a better way of judging is to divide the novel into two sections: dialogue and nondialogue. I believe that in the nondialogue, or descriptive passages the revisions are largely improvements, and that in the dialogue passages they are not. The late Jamesian style is certainly richer and more vivid, and Paris of the Second Empire glitters before us more luminously in the 1907 prose, but the dialogue is not helped by having been made more stylized and artificial. The essence of the book lies in the character of Christopher Newman and in the contrast that his directness and simplicity offer to the deviousness and snobbishness of an ancient French aristocratic family. I cannot but feel that any marked increase in the subtlety of his discriminations must make him a less forceful dramatic protagonist.

The late Jamesian style, after all, was adopted for late Jamesian characters. For Lambert Strether, who is to some extent a Christopher Newman grown middle-aged, the language of *The Ambassadors* provides a comfortable and appropriate ambience. But it is occasionally baffling to have Christopher Newman, fresh from American cutthroat business and the carnage of the Civil War, think like one of the subtle but disembodied intelligences of *The Golden Bowl*.

Swann, Male Chauvinist
and Albertine, Boy-Girl

A GREAT NOVEL should be able to survive any number of social changes. Even if the author has shown himself sympathetic to a character who seems morally flawed to our later vision, this should not affect our enjoyment of the book so long as the character is portrayed in depth. I was amused to discover on a recent rereading of *Du Côté de Chez Swann* that Proust's hero is a male chauvinist of the worst sort for whose misery I haven't the slightest sympathy. Yet my delight in his story was unimpaired.

When Swann meets Odette de Crécy he is one of those rich, middle-aged, charming bachelor dilettantes who adorned European society of the *belle époque*, with no better occupation, when not killing game on a weekend or looking at pictures in a gallery, than to chase women. Although a Jew, he is accepted in the very highest Parisian society because of his lazy amiability, his wit, and his reputation for heroism in the war against Prussia, and because, too, having no appendages, he will not embroil his hostesses in a Jewish domestic milieu. Closely modeled on Charles Haas, an exquisite socialite and adviser to rich collectors of objets d'art,

Swann was everything that Proust wanted to be himself, except that he was not an artist. He is Proust's dream — a perfect one, for instead of making the dreamer's real life seem inferior, he is possessed of a defect that makes it a hollow simulacrum of actuality: Swann is a dilettante.

There is a note of unpleasant crowing in Proust's famous apostrophe to "dear Charles Swann, whom I knew when I was still so young and you were near the grave — it is because he whom you must have thought a silly young man has made you the hero of one of his volumes that people begin to talk of you again, and that your name will perhaps live." Proust here is not unlike an English "tweeney" exclaiming over the beauty and hauteur of a royal princess and reflecting at the same time that the glory of a crown lies largely in the eye of the beholder. What is Swann, or Haas, without Proust?

But what is Proust without Swann? There is a kind of revenge for Charles Haas in the survival of his elegant person and amiable disdain in a literary immortality that seems almost to vulgarize Proust's conversion of snobbishness into art.

Swann, however, is still a male chauvinist. I turn now to Odette de Crécy. She is a high-class prostitute who maintains a pretty little house and a social life on the fringes of questionable salons. We never know her exact age, but I infer from the way men talk of her ("I had her the night MacMahon came in") that when Swann meets her, she has already had a considerable career and is in her middle or late thirties. Any reader of French fiction of the last century knows how bleak was the future of such a woman. She rarely saved enough for the day when her beauty would be gone and she was apt to end in the dreaded *hôpital*. Proust does not emphasize Odette's insecurity; he did not have to. His readers would take it for granted.

When Swann first becomes Odette's lover, he is not more than casually enamored. Love, a great love, like all such in Proust, comes only with jealousy. Once he begins to suspect her of sleeping with other men — and women — he dedicates his life to frenzied investigations. He haunts the Verdurins' salon to watch her; he follows her to their seaside place; he makes endless inquiries and even begs his friends, like Charlus, to keep an eye on her. All of his energy and emotion, and much of his thinking are devoted to this obsession. The favorite bachelor of the *gratin*, the hero of 1870, the connoisseur of Dutch painting, the friend of the Prince of Wales and the Duc d'Orleans, the only Jew ever to be elected to the Jockey Club, gives over his days and nights to this endless search for any who may have access to the nether regions of his mistress.

Is his jealousy warranted? Entirely. Why on earth should Odette be faithful? She never loves him, at least not exclusively. His erudition bores her; his social life is closed to her. He is generous with money, undoubtedly, but only for current expenses. Would he *settle* anything on her? Probably not. If she were to give up other men, where would she be when he tired of her? She has to keep her hand in. She has to be current. She and Swann never live together openly — she is too "respectable" for that — so that their liaison is strewn with opportunities for her to betray him. We are never told how long a period is covered by Swann's infatuation and despair, but it is evidently many years. At the end of the Swann Amoureux section he exclaims to himself:

To think that I've ruined years of my life, that I've even yearned for death, that I've experienced my greatest passion — for what? — for a woman who doesn't even basically appeal to me, who's not my style!

Thirty years ago, I was moved by the picture of the hero's suffering. Most readers were. It seemed to be universally agreed that no novelist had ever more vividly evoked the agony of jealousy. But today I keep wondering: why doesn't Swann marry Odette?

It is all she wants. Her infidelities are her revenge on a man who is taking advantage of her. She is not unduly sexed; one even suspects her of being cool. She would make a perfect wife for an aging man.

Yet never once does he seriously consider this obvious solution to his difficulty. He even makes the argument to himself that, married to a woman so essentially dull and commonplace, he would inevitably cease to love her! He seems to be infatuated with his own misery. He may be in love, but his love is totally selfish. He is a dilettante in human relations as in art, and if this makes him unhappy, he has nobody to thank but himself.

Now it will be argued that I am taking Swann out of his era and judging him by modern standards. *Could* a gentleman in his day marry a woman of Odette's reputation? Yes, and, of course, Swann does, although only after he has ceased to love her and presumably to legitimize his child. But when he does so — whatever his motive — peace envelops his life. He enjoys her flower arrangements, her dresses, her interior decoration. It amuses him to surround her with a kind of society. Of course, he cannot expect the duchesses of the Faubourg St. Germain to call on her, but he uses all his old social skill and tact to assemble in her parlor a little court of republican politicians. And after his death the duchesses, ironically enough, *will* call. Swann's widow becomes a leader of fashionable society. The Duchess de Guermantes will not receive Odette while Swann is alive because he was one of her faithful and has to be punished for marrying without her sanction, but after his death . . . well, one hears, does one not, that Madame Swann is charming?

Because Proust saw the relationship between Swann and Odette in depth, it does not matter that he had little or no sympathy for the plight of the prostitute in a male-dominated society. He gives us the facts; we can make our own judgments. Swann Amoureux never becomes dated. What then of the narrator, Marcel, and Albertine? But that is a different matter. It is not real.

Surely even the most devoted Proustian would have to admit that Marcel's and Albertine's is a strange affair on which to base a universal theory of love. Marcel is first seriously attracted to her when he sees her dancing with another girl in a cabaret, and Doctor Cottard points out to him that they are playing a sexual game by rubbing their breasts together. He at once drops into hell, not because his love for Albertine has been soiled but because it has been created. From now on, like Swann, he devotes himself to the job of preventing Albertine from indulging her lesbian tastes. It becomes the sole object of a hitherto idle life. He moves her into his family's flat in Paris (a curious arrangement for a "respectable" girl, even though there seems to be a precedent for it in Proust's own life) and selects friends to watch over her. Although he declines to marry her himself, it never seems to occur to him — at least until after she has fled — that his arrangement may be hurting the poor girl's chances of making a good match. Indeed, Albertine's welfare never bothers him at all. He is entirely taken up with the love inside himself. For a man's love to Proust is a totally subjective matter. It attaches itself to almost any female, depending on the circumstances of a first meeting; it grows with the unavailability, indifference, or

even scorn of the attracting woman, and it is finally brought
to its fullest intensity by jealousy, particularly jealousy of
another female.

Now, obviously, there is a homosexual underpinning to
this theory. The love of one male invert for another, in
Proust's day, concealed as it had to be from a hostile and con-
temptuous society, was born in guilt and predestined to sor-
row, and if one of the parties made love to a woman, the
jealousy of the other was hideously intensified by the element
of double betrayal. Then why not, as some have suggested,
interpret the Albertine passages by reading them as if Albertine were Albert? Because one can't. Albertine is not a simple
disguise for a young man. Proust is too good a writer for that.
She is definitely a woman. He has taken a contemporary
homosexual case history and converted it into a heterosexual
love affair. But it won't wash. One cannot call Marcel a male
chauvinist; he is not taking advantage of a woman.

I belong to the unfashionable but unrepentant persuasion
that finds the Albertine passages a serious flaw in *A la Recherche du Temps Perdu*. The last time that I read through
the seven novels I did so in reverse order. It confirmed something that I had long suspected, namely, that the narrator's
affair with Albertine acts as a drag as the work progresses.
Reading the story backward I found my interest, on the contrary, increasing in intensity until *Du Côté de Chez Swann*
provided a fitting and tremendous climax. Only in the last
third of *A L'Ombre des Jeunes Filles en Fleurs,* where the
narrator meets Albertine and her girl friends on the beach
at Balbec, did I find the process reversed.

I think that for many young and future readers the time
has come for an abbreviated version of *A la Recherche,* which
would run to 60 percent of its present length, the greatest

cuts being in the Albertine sections. Of course, the old Proust guard will be down on me. There are many who profess to find in the interminable analyses of the narrator's jealousy Proust's finest work. There are even those who decry the parties at the Guermantes' and the Verdurins' as rather old-fashioned sketches, hangovers from the nineteenth-century novel of manners, amusing to be sure, clever undoubtedly, but part of a familiar past from which the cognoscenti have long graduated. Nathalie Sarraute represents the extreme of this school. She allows herself to wonder what Proust could have thought he was doing in devoting so many thousands of words to elaborate descriptions of such obvious types as Swann, the Duchess de Guermantes, Madame Verdurin, and Doctor Cottard, and she likens the reader who enjoys such characters to his predecessor in the last century who reveled in the slick society novels of George Ohnet. But to me this is a heresy far worse than my own.

Well, those who like Proust in the entirety can always read him so. The question that I raise is whether or not a short-ened version should be made available to others. My feelings were considerably strengthened when I discovered, in reading George Painter's biography of Proust, that *A la Recherche* had originally been conceived in very much the form I sug-gest. When *Du Côté de Chez Swann* appeared in 1913 Proust contemplated only two other volumes, *Le Côté de Guer-mantes* and *Le Temps Retrouvé*. These would have included much of *A L'Ombre* and the present *Le Côté de Guermantes*, together with the quarrel between the Baron de Charlus and the Verdurins which now appears in *La Prisonnière* and the conclusions of the present *Le Temps Retrouvé*. Further pub-lication, however, was interrupted by the First World War and in the interim Proust decided to expand his original scheme by putting in the long affair with Albertine (already a projected character but not nearly so important a one) , which had been inspired by his own affair with his chauffeur, Agostinelli. According to Painter, this intensified and deepened a great work. Obviously, I disagree.

It may relieve some readers to learn that I was unable to obtain the rights for a cut Proust. That will have to wait until they pass into the public domain.

Nancy Mitford's Versailles

THE CHÂTEAU DE VERSAILLES is as popular today as it
ever was, as full of tourists as it once was of courtiers.
Yet we are told by the knowledgeable that this huge, empty,
gilded loft, hung with bad pictures and echoing with the
conned narrations of elderly guides, barely suggests the beautiful treasure palace that all Europe once regarded with wonder and awe. What then is its attraction? Could it be its mere
size, in our era of monsters? I doubt it. I think it must be the
fantastic political concept of Versailles that keeps pulling in
the crowds, the outrageous concept that such a Kafka-like
nightmare of royal bureaucracy was any way to govern a
nation. Before this huge cemetery of dead and unworkable
ideas one can only stand transfixed, with an occasional uneasy twitch at the thought that it may *not,* after all, be quite
as dead as one has assumed.

The fascination has been as great to the historian as to
the tourist. Professors have always been infuriated by Versailles. They have condemned it as frivolous, boring, artificial, inhuman, or just plain ridiculous. It sometimes seems as
if they could not bear the idea that Louis XV and Madame
de Pompadour might have had more fun out of life than the
faculties of Harvard or Ohio State. And the moralists, of

course, never tire of denouncing the iniquities of the *Parc aux Cerfs*. But the defenders of Versailles have not been much better. We have seen, on the shelves of old libraries, those large volumes with engraved illustrations protected by onion paper, which purport to turn the daughters and mistresses of the French monarchs into so many noble English matrons of Edwardian society. Between the comminations and the false praise, one may prefer the comminations.

If Versailles was a disease, it was certainly a catching one. The idea of it permeated the whole of the *Ile de France,* where smaller chateaux were thrown up everywhere in emulation of the sovereign; and it spread out to ruin the exchequers of European capitals. It was as if the neurosis of Louis XIV had transformed nature itself from its natural tangle of disorder into a great compound of straight alleys, huge parks and formal gardens. The Sun King detested disorder and probably detested mankind. He may have identified all who were not courtiers or mannequins with the smelly mob that invaded his nursery during the civil wars of his minority. His revenge was nothing less than to re-create the world in his image. He tried to impose order on chaos by turning his kingdom into a gigantic boarding school under the ever vigorous eye of a never-sleeping headmaster. Anybody he could not see was probably up to no good.

There was an overwhelming negation of life in such a philosophy, or such a psychosis, whichever one chooses to call it; but it is still possible to see King Louis in the light of a bewildered modern man trying in vain to impose unity upon multiplicity. If men were to conform, to become "one," they had to be turned into dolls, into children. And, indeed, human beings under the Versailles system tended to become childlike. If they were put back into school, how else could they develop? They became petty, gossipy, obsessed with small prizes and small distinctions. In all their bowing and curtsying they were like boys in close order drill. They have been branded as artificial, but they were children of nature in the candor of their egotism and their rapacity.

Versailles offers a lugubrious parallel to some aspects of our civilization. There is a kind of conformity in our very insistence on innovation. Universities, governments, works of art are judged by standards of "relevancy" and "meaningfulness" as stiff as the unities of Boileau. And on the other side of the coin, Versailles is the Pentagon itself. The system created by the Sun King was a monster that got out of control. His unfortunate descendant, Louis XVI, faced with a chorus of demands that he cut down its huge wasteful bureaucracy, cried out that it was impossible. In the same way our bureaucracy was incapable of untangling a war that nobody wanted.

Few historians have addressed themselves to the question: *why* did Versailles work? Why did it dominate Europe for a whole century? Why did it accomplish what it set out to accomplish, i.e., to render the peerage impotent and oblige them to exchange their swords for ribbons? Why did thousands of rich and independent nobles desert their beautiful chateaux all over France to huddle in small rooms in the palace of a monarch who never included them in his cabinet? Why did the princesses of France refuse the hands of sovereigns in order to remain old maids under the paternal roof? Why was exile from court to his own duchy regarded by even the richest duke as a fate worse than death?

Nancy Mitford claims that it was simply because life at Versailles was so delightful. She has scant patience with the pedants, whose grapes she finds very sour. It seems to be her view that most modern academicians, brought up amid the horrors of industrial civilization and shackled to the burden of a public conscience, can no longer even conceive of the delights of a true epicureanism. She may be right.

Miss Mitford has come to history by way of fiction. In 1954 she wrote a biography of Madame de Pompadour and in 1966 a study of Louis XIV at Versailles. She seems to have brought a new talent to the study of history: that of the sophisticated, worldly-wise observer, who is able to penetrate old archives with a fresh eye for qualities in the dead that she is specially qualified to recognize. Miss Mitford permits herself to doubt the evidence of the Duc de Luynes as to the reputed wit and high spirits of his friend, Queen Maria Leczinska, pointing out that people lucky enough to belong to the circle of royal personages are fond of letting it be understood that the latter are less dull than they look. She is probably thinking of some aunt or cousin who was once in waiting to Queen Mary.

Her point of view is unabashedly aristocratic. In speaking of the plumbing at Versailles she compares it with that of Buckingham Palace in 1923, when, after waiting for hours in the long line of vehicles to be presented, she found only a chamber pot behind a curtain in the ladies' room. Many of Miss Mitford's friends in Paris are descendants of people who lived at Versailles and are probably not unlike them. One feels that if she found herself transported back there, she would, with a little practice, know how to conduct herself, even under the exacting eye of that fierce little diarist peer, the Duc de Saint-Simon, whose work, incidentally, she has edited.

Yet she is no champion of her protagonists. She is not in the least interested in defending them from the indictments under which history has almost buried them. She makes short work of Louis XIV as a statesman and ruler. She finds it perfectly obvious that his border warfare was a simple waste of lives and money and his religious policy a bane to French commerce. She is equally sure that Madame de Pompadour made a ninny of herself when she jumped into the game of power politics and persuaded Louis XV to convert his family's traditional rivalry with the House of Austria into a disastrous alliance.

She is no less hard on personal failings. She notes that the Sun King believed in a God who objected more to a single night of adultery than to the slaughter of a battalion of men, and concludes that Christianity was a closed book to him. She is not devoid of sentiment — she has her favorites: Madame de Montespan (who, consulting the occult, said that she had time for only one black mass), the charming Prince de Conti, the Pompadour herself — but she keeps it well under the control of her probing reason. Indeed, the hard, clear light that she casts upon the court of France seems itself an eighteenth-century illumination.

Her job, as she describes it, is to describe the amusing things that people did at Versailles and the beautiful things that they caused to be created. That, after all, was the point of the place. She sets it before us with brevity and vividness and wit. We feel some of the hypnotic fascination of living constantly close to the source of absolute power; we become aware of the fantastic interior decoration, the sweeping magnificent gardens. We even feel some of the strange attraction of the constant show of thousands of well-dressed, well-trained people knowing just what to do and when and how to do it.

It is all rather horrible, yet intriguingly horrible. By cutting away the world, the small things become grotesquely magnified and grotesquely interesting. Life has the daily tenseness of a small academy redeemed in the eyes of its students by their constant sense of being the center of the universe. For at Versailles nobody ever doubted that that was where they were.

Is what Miss Mitford does worth doing? Certainly, if history is worth doing at all. Nobody can understand the seventeenth and eighteenth centuries in Europe without understanding the phenomenon of the Versailles system. Miss Mitford illuminates the relentless, plodding, barely human monarch who reared this fantastic dolls' house and created the elaborate machinery of its etiquette and the woman who, a quarter of a century after his death, saved it in the only way it could be saved, by enveloping it in an enchanting fairy-tale mist in which its cruder outlines could be blurred. After the Pompadour, a great dullness fell over Versailles. It was time for the vulgar excesses of Madame DuBarry — and of the Revolution.

Dreiser's Love of America

THEODORE DREISER EMERGES from W. A. Swanberg's
biography as a violent, opinionated, bigoted, unlovable
man whose disregard for truth led him into slander, whose
greed involved him in plagiarism, and whose cranky, per-
verse temper sank him at last in the bogs of communism.
What a Christmas package this book would make, boxed with
Mark Schorer's life of Sinclair Lewis, for those who like to
see that generation of American men of letters disparaged!
One is not surprised to find that the two subjects disliked
each other and once actually came to fisticuffs at a public dinner. Like F. Scott Fitzgerald and Dylan Thomas, they rarely
disappointed their scandal-loving audiences.

Lewis and Dreiser shared not only faults of personality, but
faults as writers as well. Their styles, at worst, were flat and
obvious, their tastes questionable, their points too heavily
made. But their differences were even greater. Lewis had a
sense of humor, and Dreiser none. Lewis hated the world that
he attacked, and Dreiser loved it. Lewis was at heart a journalist, and Dreiser was at heart — at his best and worst — an
artist.

Alfred Kazin has pointed out that people keep trying to

"explain" Dreiser. How is it that such a bad writer could have been such a great one? The Swanberg book answers every question *but* that. I suggest that there may be two answers: one, that urban life in America in the first two decades of our century corresponded to Dreiser's concept of it as a jungle, and, two, that he liked jungles, or at least that he liked the spectacle of ferocity, the drama of the struggle for survival. Perhaps what I am saying is that he liked life in the raw — or life in the raw as he conceived it. In this respect, his true literary brother is not Lewis but Zola. I find in their work, for all their naiveté, even for all their occasional vulgarity, a contagious enthusiasm for their subject matter which distinguishes them from all other novelists of the past hundred years.

They entertain us, even when they most appall us. Sister Carrie, with an aching back, working twelve hours a day in a shoe factory, Hurstwood degenerating from prosperity into beggary, Clyde Griffiths plotting the murder of his pregnant girl friend, are somehow never depressing. Even when Dreiser is at his grimmest there is always something so vital in his curiosity, so exciting in his sense of the dramatic (in which I include the hammy) that, heartless as it sounds, one is more fascinated than depressed. Zola in his most unspeakable scenes — the murder and mayhem in *La Terre,* the filth and promiscuity of mining life in *Germinal* — holds one arrested in much the same way. In reading the *Rougon-Macquart* novels one even sometimes suspects a deficiency in one's human sympathy. How else could one read of such human degradation without a revulsion and disgust quite inconsistent with even the smallest idea of pleasure?

I think that Kazin has caught the reader's reaction to Dreiser very aptly when he compares his urban backgrounds with the paintings of Edward Hopper. The emotion conveyed consists in "exactly this *surprise of attachment* to the world that so often dwarfs us." And as Lloyd Goodrich has said, in his turn, of Hopper: "With all its realism Hopper's art has a strong strain of romantic emotion . . . the vastness, monotony and loneliness of the city have seldom been as intensely conveyed. But the final emotion is affirmative: clear morning sunlight, stillness and a sense of solitude that is poignant yet serene."

What it boils down to is that Dreiser imbues his principal characters with much of his own attachment to life. He conveys to us the appeal of things whose very repulsiveness he delights in underlining. The society that Clyde Griffiths wishes to achieve seems as sterile as any society drawn by Lewis, but where in Lewis one would simply laugh at it, in Dreiser one yearns with Clyde for the banal, snobbish, philistine merchants' world of Lycurgus. It is so infinitely preferable to the world of the workers. If life is worth anything, a comfortable life must be worth something more.

Dreiser's philosophy was as simple as were his enthusiasms. It is summed up by Mollenhauer in *The Financier:*

Life to him, as to every other man of large practical knowledge and insight, was an inexplicable tangle. What were you going to do about the so-called morals and precepts of the world? This man Stener fancied that he was dishonest, and that he, Mollenhauer, was honest. He was here, self-convicted of sin, pleading to him, Mollenhauer, as he would to a righteous, unstained saint. As a matter of fact, Mollenhauer knew that he was simply shrewder, more far-seeing, more calculating, not less dishonest. Stener was lacking in force and brains — not morals. This lack was his principal crime. There were people who believed in some esoteric standard of right — some ideal of conduct absolutely and very far removed from practical life; but he had never seen them practice it save to their own financial (not moral — he would not say that) destruction. They were never significant, practical men who clung to these fatuous ideals. They were always poor, nondescript, negligible dreamers.

Frank Cowperwood, the hero of *The Financier* and *The Titan*, is admirable to Dreiser because he accepts the universe without lamentations and seeks to grab as big a chunk of it as he can. He does not obtain lasting happiness, for lasting happiness is not there to obtain. He is the perfect lord of the jungle, for he is as strong and beautiful as a tawny lion, and, like that lion, he kills no more than he needs. Cowperwood is devoid of meanness, of snobbery, of the least smallness of character. He goes from fortune to fortune and from woman to woman, satisfying all of his desires and all of his appetites, but with a minimum of damage to others. He is Dreiser's fantasy, his Tarzan, his James Bond.

It is interesting that Dreiser seemed to lose his enthusiasm for life in America in direct proportion to the growth of policing by the federal government of such financial pirates as Cowperwood. He evidently cared less for a world where his titans were muzzled. The jungle, he must have felt, should either be let grow wild or else cleared out altogether, which may be why he ended up as a Communist. His main preoccupation was with the social struggle, not with its ultimate solution. In later years, when he went in for political theorizing, he became didactic and dull.

I believe that Dreiser was at his finest at the outset of his career, before the American urban world grew socially conscious and his own disposition worse. His first novel, *Sister Carrie*, is a perfect determinist work of fiction, for the characters respond to stimuli, without, like Cowperwood, overpowering their environment and without, like Jennie Gerhardt, surrendering to it. The plot is geometrically neat; in the end the two principal characters have changed places with each other on the social ladder. Carrie and Hurstwood carry out this slow but ineluctable operation in a cold, grey urban atmosphere of total impersonality and amorality. She starts in the dreary streets of Chicago; he ends in the drearier ones of New York. The riches and luxuries that one gains and the other loses are always seen from the simplest possible point of view: that of the deprived shop-window gazer. They must be attained because they are all that life offers. It may perfectly well be that possession will bring disenchantment, but the man in the street will always take his chances with disenchantment. He knows that there are worse things.

There is no feeling in *Sister Carrie* of a disapproving author or that Hurstwood is doing wrong in betraying his wife or even in stealing money from his employers' safe. He has simply, in the latter instance, made a tactical mistake that will ultimately cost him his life, and the wonderful horror of this moment in the story is that he knows it. When he obeys that sudden impulse and when the safe clicks fatally closed, he feels his ruin. The rest of his story is his inevitable degradation, from one poor job to a worse one, from drink to beggary. He is too old to recoup. He has lived for too many years on smiles and good fellowship as the manager of a fashionable bar. He has allowed himself to forget, in that fatal moment, that behind those smiles there is only steel and stone, that there are no second chances that one can make for oneself.

Carrie, on the other hand, although of mediocre talent, is endowed with one invaluable asset: the realization that she owes nothing to the men who keep her. Their only function is to support her until she is able to support herself in a more agreeable profession. With a pleasant voice and the knack of wearing clothes smartly, she gets a start in the musical comedy world, and she is well on her way to becoming a minor star as the book ends. Until just before the end of the novel she seems perfectly satisfied. The disillusionment with the contents of the shop window is by no means an immutable law.

Lewis would have shown the shop window full of tinsel and gaudy gimcracks that would have come apart in the deluded purchaser's hands as soon as he was out in the street. But Dreiser, like Zola, knew the joys of indiscriminate coveting and the satisfactions of hollow possession. Had he not been a faithful determinist and had he allowed a deus ex machina to rescue Hurstwood from the gutter with an unexpected legacy, Hurstwood would have been happy again. What makes Hurstwood wretched is poverty, not Hurstwood. If a man can once get his hands on money, like Cowperwood, like Carrie, unlike Clyde Griffiths, unlike Hurstwood, well, even if he doesn't have *lasting* happiness, he has about as much as this world offers. And here is the point, always the point in Dreiser: this world offers quite a lot.

But then, in the final pages, for no reason that I can make out, Dreiser reverses himself. Carrie is *not* going to be happy, after all. She is a creature doomed to unhappiness because she is caught up in the endless search for beauty. Dreiser seems to be saying here that because her standards will become higher and higher, she will be perpetually disappointed in life. Instead of being content with musical comedy, she will long to be a serious actress. But so long as she is capable of serious acting, and apparently she is, is not that the only route to abiding happiness?

The final paragraph of the book is sheer drivel.

Oh, Carrie, Carrie! Oh, blind strivings of the human heart! Onward, onward, it saith, and where beauty leads, there it follows.

Whether it be the tinkle of a lone sheep bell o'er some quiet landscape, or the glimmer of beauty in sylvan places, or the show of soul in some passing eye, the heart knows and makes answer, following. It is when the feet weary and hope seems vain that the heartaches and the longings arise. Know, then, that for you is neither surfeit nor content. In your rocking chair, by your window dreaming, shall you long, alone. In your rocking chair, by your window, shall you dream such happiness as you may never feel.

It is a curious ending, for two reasons: one, as already indicated, I do not see why it is so bad to dream such happiness; and, two, it had not occurred to me that Carrie was that kind of a dreamer.

An American Tragedy also has a confusing ending. The long trial section, comprising almost one quarter of the whole novel, adds little or nothing to the tragedy. It simply tells the story of Clyde's struggle with the forces of justice, or of injustice, and how he is sentenced to death and executed, not for what he has actually done — allowing Roberta to drown — but for something that he has not done — hitting her over the head with an oar and pushing her in the water.

There seems to be an argument in this that Clyde was not legally guilty of murder in the first degree but was the victim of a politically ambitious district attorney who doctored the evidence. From this Dreiser deduces some vague ameliorization of Clyde's moral guilt. Clyde is the victim, in the last analysis, not merely of his prosecutor but of capitalist society in the United States. The trouble with Dreiser's reasoning is that Clyde is already both morally and legally guilty of murder before the district attorney has even learned of his existence. He has lured Roberta away from home and taken her to a deep and lonely part of a lake at night with every intention of drowning her. Then he experiences a change of heart. The boat capsizes, accidentally it is true, but he leaves Roberta, whose inability to swim has formed an essential part of his plot, to drown. Having thus deliberately and maliciously placed her in danger of her life, he has imposed upon himself the duty to rescue her. The neglect of this duty is surely murder.

But in a larger sense Dreiser has already shown that Clyde is the victim of society. His foolish Evangelist father, his itinerant rootless life, his lack of formal education, his exposure in youth to the cynicism and immorality of a large hotel staff, and finally, the the agonizing contrast in Lycurgus of his poverty and low social status with the wealth and prominence of his uncle's family — all these have been fatal elements in his development. Clyde kills because his upbringing has made him a man who would murder rather than lose the money and social position that are suddenly and unexpectedly placed within his greedy grasp. The trial section of the novel, with its constant emphasis on morals, deprives the book of some of the power of *Sister Carrie*.

For the shock of *Sister Carrie* to the reading public in 1900 was not, I suspect, because it dealt with a kept woman, or even with a kept woman who became successful. Carrie does not owe her ultimate success to prostitution but to her stage career. The shock must have come from the fact that none of the principal characters ever face the moral issues implicit in their acts. Drouet is not troubled about seducing a country virgin; Hurstwood has few scruples about leaving his wife and family or taking Drouet's mistress; and Carrie herself seems to have no qualms about living with either of her lovers. The moral issue of fornication barely exists in the book, as it barely existed for the Drouets, Hurstwoods, and Carries of yesteryear and today. Dreiser believed that morals were the perquisites of the middle and upper classes.

His world seems closer to our own than the worlds of his contemporary novelists because he adopted none of the moral fashions of his day.

Indeed, one would not even be sure of the date of the action of *Sister Carrie* if the author did not clearly supply it. The novel opens in the year 1889 and continues into the mid-nineties. Similarly, it is difficult to date the action of *An American Tragedy*, which is probably the early 1920s. There are few descriptions in either novel of clothes or interiors and almost no echoes of the voice of prevailing society, the "taste makers" of the day. Dreiser tosses out late Victorian prudery along with late Victorian hats. He concentrates on how the big city will appear to a working girl who has left her family in the country, to a drummer who lives on "cheek," to a bar manager who makes his career on smiles and compliments, to a factory worker who glimpses the residential area of town. It is a dark, cold, dangerous world, but its darkness makes the gaudiest chandelier seem glittering, and its cold makes the most vulgar plush seem warm. What have such people, caught up in the simple business of survival, to do with a code of morality drawn up by those who are safe from danger? What have such struggles *ever* had to do with such codes? What do they have to do with them in our own day? Dreiser, the least intellectual of our great novelists, was always aware of the deep sea of apathy under the waves of current opinions.

Racine and Port-Royal

SAINTE-BEUVE SET about his task of writing the history of
the seventeenth-century monastery at Port-Royal with the
deliberate intention of creating his monument in literary
history, consciously likening himself to Gibbon. And to some
extent he succeeded. *Port-Royal* is a great work of history.
But it is not the inspiring religious work that it was originally intended to be, for the simple reason that Sainte-Beuve
lost his faith in the writing of it. The more he learned of the
lives of the ascetic priests and nuns of the Jansenist persuasion, the less he admired them. That they had utter courage
and utter faith was unquestionable. That they were above
worldly things, superior even to the smallest aspects of materialism, was equally clear. Spiritually they were noble, and
in their relations with their fellow men they were cheerful,
unselfish, and compassionate. But theirs was a terrible God.

According to their creed, man had been irredeemably lost
by Adam in his fall from grace, at least insofar as man's own
efforts to reacquire grace were concerned. Salvation de-
pended entirely on God, who would choose which souls to
save. This choice might sometimes be manifested by the de-
scent of grace to an individual. But man could not dispose
God to choose him, by prayer, by faith, or by deed. God's

choice was unalterable, predestined. Every man, dead, living, or unborn, was already damned or saved.

Now this might have been a tolerable doctrine to the greater Catholic community of the seventeenth century had the Jansenists taught that God usually exercised his choice in favor of salvation. But they did not. Heaven to them was a very exclusive club. It seems almost incredible today that such noble men and women could have wanted to warp the Christian doctrine into anything so arid and cruel. But they did. Why, then, did they bother to be ascetic, if it did them no good? If self-sacrifice and charity went for nothing? The answer is that they *enjoyed* being ascetic. It gave them the feeling that grace had descended on them, that they were chosen. Once they felt the infusion of grace, they had no further interest in anything but union with God. A monastic life was not a mortification of the flesh in the interests of future reward; it was an anticipation of those rewards. The joy of heaven was already felt in Port-Royal.

It is possible to understand the appeal of such a faith to the little group of those who believed in their own selection. But what was its power over a lusty young man like Jean Racine, after he had broken away from his devout Jansenist family and was frankly enjoying the abominations of art and love in Paris, both with the greatest success? If he were damned, might he not as well enjoy himself? If he were saved, might he not as well enjoy himself? But the doctrine of the Jansenists was insidious. How could he be sure that his rare moments of revived religious feeling, even in Paris, even in bed with the actress Marie de Champmeslé, might not be signs of grace? And if this was so, if he was actually one of the saved, might he not still damn himself by turning away deliberately from God? Salvation was predestined, yes, but God was all-powerful. If man had fallen once, might not even a saved man fall again? Might not God be *outraged* into changing His mind and choice?

I do not believe that it is fanciful to identify the dark God of the Jansenists with the offstage character who dominates the action in four of Racine's greatest tragedies: the merciless sultan of *Bajazet;* the bloodthirsty high priest of *Iphigénie;* the Venus of *Phèdre;* and the Jehovah of *Athalie.* In each of these plays the invisible character controls those whom we do see and makes the decision, so to speak, between the elect and the damned. We can trace in them the growing influence on the troubled playwright of his nagging sense of a watching deity, cruel, arbitrary, omnipotent, inescapable.

Amurat, the dreaded sultan in *Bajazet,* is away from Constantinople, where the action of the play occurs, engaged in laying siege to Babylon and resisting a Persian army sent to raise this siege. It seems an opportune moment for a palace revolution at home. The wily Vizier, Acomat, plots to depose his monarch and rule through his successor, Bajazet; the latter, a prisoner, hopes that the plot will bring him liberty and love, while the ferocious Sultana, Roxane, deludes herself with the belief that Bajazet will marry her and continue her rule. But in the tense, breathless, intrigue-ridden atmosphere of the seraglio we feel the note of doom. We are sure that Amurat will be victorious, that he will return. The others may writhe and twist; there is no escaping his vengeance. And at last he sends his messenger before him.

> *Orcan, le plus fidèle à servir ses desseins,*
> *Né sous le ciel brûlant des plus noirs Africains.*

The Sultan knows — he has always known — just what they are all up to, and in the end Bajazet and Roxane are strangled, and the Vizier is seen undertaking a hopeless resistance.

The curtain falls on a stricken court, ready to fall on its knees before the returning monarch. Amurat is a terrible, remorseless destiny.

I believe that when he wrote *Bajazet* Racine must have been at the very peak of his resentment against the doctrines of Port-Royal. He could never bring himself altogether to reject the Jansenist deity, but he was not yet afraid to show him as he was. If the sultan was God, the world was the darker for it. Roxane must die, but her passion is beautiful, as is the love and nobility of Bajazet and the fine fidelity of Atalide. Amurat may reign forever, but only in blackness, when he has extinguished all the lights. Racine had begun to identify his poetic genius with the spirit of man, as opposed to the spirit of God. There was a Promethean quality in his defiance.

But the gloom is always there. For how can the damned ever be happy? Calchas, the invisible high priest of *Iphigénie,* professes to represent the gods in demanding the victim whom they have designated, but as he is the sole interpreter of their wishes, he is in the position of being God himself. A victim he must have, and not all the agony of Agamemnon, or the fury of his wife, or even the wrath of Achilles will prevail against him. The only thing that saves Iphigénie in the end is that a substitute victim is found in Ériphile. Unlike the sultan's family in *Bajazet,* the House of Atreus is allowed to escape the doom and be happy, but only when another throat has been found to satisfy Calchas's knife.

There is a note of faintly unpleasant moralizing in this tragedy. Racine seems almost to be trying to justify the gods. They are not, it appears, quite as bloodthirsty as we might have thought. They never really wanted the innocent Iphigénie; they wanted a woman of Helen's blood, her bastard cousin, the wicked Ériphile. This unhappy creature, who does not appear in the Greek version, has been invented by the playwright and endowed with bad character so that we need not regret her sacrifice. The deities, or deity, are not as cruel as they were in *Bajazet;* they seem to have developed some dim ethical values. They kill, but they kill the guilty, not the innocent.

Ériphile is a lost soul, one of the unelected; she is at the mercy of her own fate and powerless to do anything to avert it. Her life has been one of hardship and humiliation. She has been made a prisoner of war and finds herself a victim of Venus, for against her will she falls passionately in love with her captor, Achilles. She wishes to stay away from the scene of his marriage to Iphigénie, but she has been drawn ineluctably to Aulis by a secret force or fate within herself:

Une secrète voix m'ordonna de partir.

So far it appears that Ériphile must suffer simply because her destiny requires that she must suffer, a Jansenist situation. But Racine could not yet accept the full Jansenist position. If he was willing in *Bajazet* to face the case of men and women of free will going down to defeat before an implacable God through no fault of their own, he was now tempering his position by endowing that God or gods with some aspect of justice and at the same time tainting the nonelect with a degree of guilt. Ériphile is not a puppet of the gods when she warns Calchas of the flight of Iphigénie and her mother. She seems here to be acting of her own free will and showing herself thoroughly depraved.

In his next and most famous tragedy, *Phèdre,* Racine moves at last to the extreme Jansenist position: his heroine is a lost soul through no fault of her own. Venus has caused her damnation, and no reason is ascribed for Venus's hostility. No reason need be; Venus is a goddess.

It must be understood that Phedre's sin consists essentially in her incestuous love for her stepson. Modern readers are inclined to find her evil only in her false accusation of her stepson. Why should she be held responsible for a passion that enters her heart against her will and to which she gives no outward expression (other than to her confidant) until she is led to believe that her husband is dead? And is the love for a stepson incest, anyway, in our eyes? But to understand the play, we must recognize that it is the passion and not the false witnessing that, to the eyes of the protagonist and of all the other characters, constitutes her real guilt.

Let us consider step by step whether Phèdre is really guilty of framing Hippolyte. When she first meets him, she is the devoted young wife of Thesée, a middle-aged libertine whom she has redeemed from his amorous ways. It seems a good marriage, despite the discrepancy of ages, and it is endowed with issue. Phèdre has presumably had no reason to consider herself subject to the attraction of younger men; she is contented with her lot. But Hippolyte strikes her where she has no guard: in the very bosom of her family. He is particularly irresistible in being the ideal of which her husband is now only the faded and shabby copy. For Hippolyte is not only young and strong and beautiful, he is chaste. He is Thesée without the years or the vices. Venus has played a singularly nasty trick on a would-be honest wife.

Yet Phèdre struggles valiantly with her gripping passion. She avoids Hippolyte; she even pretends to be his enemy and exiles him. Thesée brings him home again. She offers sacrifices to Venus — hecatombs — to no avail. At last she sickens and hopes to escape further guilt by dying. Oenone, her faithful old nurse, extracts her guilty secret, but only because her mistress believes it to be a death-bed confession. Oenone is almost as horrified by this passion as is its victim! There is no effort on either side to minimize its criminal aspect.

And now the news is brought of Thesée's death. This at once takes the crime out of the situation, perhaps even the incest. Hippolyte has always avoided women, so presumably Phèdre has no rival. She and he are probably close to the same age (though this has been clouded by generations of famous older actresses taking the part). What could be more appropriate than that the young widowed queen regent should seek the hand and protection of the first prince of the blood? Might it not avoid civil war? Such an alliance would seem almost a dynastic duty.

But Venus has more tricks up her sleeve. Hippolyte unexpectedly rejects his stepmother's advances, and with a scornful violence that reduces Phèdre to total despair. On top of this Thesée reappears, not dead at all. In her shame and panic Phèdre allows herself to be persuaded by Oenone to throw the blame of the first advance on her proud and censorious stepson. Oenone assures her that Thesée will let Hippolyte off easily. After all, consider his own past! Phèdre collapses and leaves the dirty job to the nurse.

This, then, aside from her passion, is her sole crime. It would be a wicked one, indeed, had her will power not been reduced to jelly by sexual frustration, gnawing guilt, sickness, and the most mortifying of humiliations. Yet even so she recovers herself quickly and goes to her husband to implore him to forgive Hippolyte, prepared, if necessary, to confess what she has done. But Venus has a final trick. Thesée flings in her face that Hippolyte is in love with Aricie! Phèdre is now paralyzed, temporarily incapable of further action. By the time she has regained control of herself Hippolyte is dead. Still, after taking poison she manages to stagger into her husband's presence to clear with her dying breath the slandered youth. She then expires, despised by her husband, by the gods, and by herself.

And by Racine? To some extent. She is a lost soul, and lost souls, by definition, must be bad. It does not matter that they are without fault. What about pagans and unbaptized infants and all those millions of humans who lived before Christ? Racine felt their plight; he felt it passionately, because he must have always wondered if he did not share it. I believe that he had now come to identify all that stood between man and the uninterrupted contemplation of God as dangerous distractions, and art, his own art, as the most dangerous of all. Phèdre, the character *and* the play, the heroine and all her beautiful lines, was damnable simply because she was not God.

So what could he do but give up the theater? Give it up and marry a dull *dévote* and become the king's historiographer? It is almost enough to make one have a sneaking sympathy with the Sun King's later outrageous persecution of the Jansenists to consider that they had suppressed Racine at the very apex of his playwrighting career! At first he quibbled with them. He tried to have his cake and eat it too by asking his friends at Port-Royal if *Phèdre* were not a moral play. Why then, they retorted, had he introduced the love of Hippolyte and Aricie, not to be found in Euripides? But if Racine tried, understandably, to save a bit of his past from their sweeping condemnations, he was obedient about the future. No other tragedy would come from his pen.

Until, of course, Madame de Maintenon commissioned

him to write a play for the girl students at St. Cyr. There was no refusing the king's morganatic wife. Racine wrote *Esther,* a charming charade. Even Port-Royal could not have been disturbed. But when Madame de Maintenon asked for a second piece, he succumbed to his old devil and wrote *Athalie.* How could he not? It was as if he had been put to bed with Venus and told only to say his prayers.

The unseen character in this tragedy is none other than Jehovah, God, the *Dieu des Juifs.* The Queen of Juda, Athalie, is the unelected, lost soul. She is the protagonist, and God the antagonist, in this final drama of the great Jansenist poet. With the death and damnation of Athalie, Racine abandoned his muse and dedicated his working days to the king and his soul to the terrible deity of Port-Royal.

It may be argued that Athalie, unlike Phèdre, is certainly a wicked character and that the god who condemns her has considerable justification. Did she not murder her own offspring? Did she not plot the assassination of young Joas? But here again Racine goes out of his way to place his doomed character in the most favorable possible moral light. Athalie has slaughtered her children in a time of violent religious warfare when members of the royal family were hacking each other to pieces without quarter. Had she not seen her own parents butchered? Had she not sworn to avenge them, even against her own flesh and blood? She is convinced that her children were worshipers of a false god and that by exterminating them she has not only avenged her parents, but reestablished the true religion. She points out that she has brought order out of chaos, that she has ruled wisely and well. Her ends, she maintains, have justified her means. And as far as Joas is concerned, she wavers back and forth between good and bad intentions and finally offers, in apparent good faith, to bring him up in her palace as her heir. When she speaks to the boy, it is with some of the gentleness of the first act Phèdre:

> *"Venez dans mon palais, vous y verrez ma gloire,"*
> and
> *"Dieu veut que toute heure on prie, on le contemple?"*

Just as the real sin of Phèdre is her guilty passion for, and not her betrayal of, Hippolyte, so the real crime of Athalie is her heresy, and not her murders. Phèdre is the victim of Venus, and there is nothing she can do about it. And Athalie is quite correct when she cries out that she has been destroyed by the God of the Jews operating within herself to deliver her to her enemies:

> *C'est toi qui me flattait d'une vengeance aisée,*
> *M'as vingt fois dans un jour a moi-même opposée.*

What we are up against, as usual, is predestination. Phèdre and Athalie are sin-ridden creatures because they have been predestined to be so. They cannot save themselves, and they cannot be saved. At the same time they represent all that is most sensitive and feeling and artistic in this world. Racine's final sacrifice to Port-Royal was to destroy all his notes for the final edition of his plays. Not only did God not want them; He did not want them improved.

In Search of Innocence:
Henry Adams and John La Farge
in the South Seas

WHEN MARIAN HOOPER ADAMS took her fatal dose of
potassium cyanide on December 6, 1885, she almost
smashed the life out of her husband as well. Suicide makes a
clean sweep of the past and present; worst of all, it repudiates
love. Until that day Henry Adams might have reasonably
considered that his life was successful. He had not, to be sure,
been President of the United States, like his grandfather and
great-grandfather, or Minister to England, like his father, but
he had been a brilliant and popular teacher of medieval history at Harvard, a successful editor of the *North American
Review,* a noted biographer and essayist, and he was in process of completing his twelve-volume history of the Jefferson
and Madison administrations which even such a self-depreca-
tor as he himself must have suspected would one day be a
classic. But above all this, far above, he had believed that he
and his wife were happy. Now he had to face the fact that she
had not been, perhaps had never been, and that his marriage
had been an illusion.

Recovering from the first shock, he took a trip to Japan with his friend John La Farge. Then he went back to Washington, and worked for three laborious years to finish his history and prepare it for the press. After that, at last, he was free. He had neither child nor job, and his means were ample. In August of 1890 he and La Farge sailed again from San Francisco for a voyage of indefinite duration to the South Seas. Many writers have speculated on why he went. One Adams scholar told me that he had once made a list of seventeen possible motives. Suffice it to say that Adams had reached the end of one life and was wondering if another could exist for him.

La Farge was the perfect traveling companion. Ernest Samuels has described him as an original genius with a Faustian nature who maintained a large, devoutly Catholic family in Newport while he kept bachelor's hall in New York. He was delighted to explore the Pacific at Adams' expense, leaving his family and creditors behind. A master in oils and water color, he could also talk and write exuberantly on all the subjects that he reproduced.

The Pacific opened up a new dimension of color. La Farge's journal is a hymn to the sea and air. He taught Adams to observe the exquisite clearness of the butterfly blue of the sky, laid on between clouds and shading down to a white faintness in the distance where the haze of ocean covered up the turquoise. He made him peer down into the water, framed in the opening of a ship's gangway, and see how the sapphire blue seemed to pour from it. He pointed out the varieties of pink and lilac and purple and rose in the clouds at sunset. Adams never learned to be more than an amateur painter, but his vision was immensely sharpened.

They went first to Oahu where they made the discovery

that every other island was to confirm: the charm of the
Pacific declined in exact proportion to the penetration of the
white man. It was not until October, when they landed on
Upolu in the Samoas, that they came in touch with a culture
that was still largely unspoiled. The natives, grave and cour-
teous, greeted them benevolently and made them feel immediately at home. They drank the ceremonial *kawa,* muddy
water mixed with grated root, which left a persistent little
aftertaste that no amount of coconut milk could quite wash
away, and they watched the *siva,* a dance performed by girls
naked to the waist, their dark skins shining with coconut oil,
seated cross-legged with garlands of green leaves around their
heads and loins. The girls chanted as they swayed and
stretched out their arms in all directions; they might have
come out of the nearby sea. La Farge's spectacles quivered
with emotion, but Adams was able to assure his correspondent Elizabeth Cameron that nothing in the song or dance
suggested the least impropriety. Again and again he was to
comment on such evidences of Rousseauistic innocence.

Samoa was ruled by Malietoa, the puppet king of the western nations' consuls, but Mataafa, the deposed monarch, still
held the loyalty of most of the population. Adams and La
Farge, scrupulously neutral, called on both and learned a
concept of aristocracy beside which Adams felt like the son
of a camel driver degraded to the position of stable boy in
Spokane West Center. For the real art of the Samoans was
social. Even the breeding among the chiefs was systematic.
They selected their wives for strength and form, with the re-
sult that the principal families enjoyed a physical as well as
a social superiority. Yet at the same time Adams observed
that the society was basically communistic. All of the presents that he and La Farge lavishly handed out to their hosts:

umbrellas, silk scarfs, gowns, cigars, were soon seen parading about the villages on strangers. Every chief was basically a poor man because he was obliged to share what he had.

In Apia the travelers found the first corrosive effects of European influence. In the big *siva* organized in their honor by the American consul, the girls deferred to missionary prejudices by wearing banana leaves over their breasts. Adams was at once reminded of the world and the devil. To-day we may be amused at his surprise that the Polynesian standard of female beauty should be more in the body than the face, but we must remember that in 1890 the face was all that American women exposed. He and La Farge, how-ever, did not carry their preference for old Samoan customs to the point of adopting the native want of costume. They feared ridicule, not to mention mosquitoes.

Everywhere they asked their hosts endless questions about customs, families, and religion and everywhere they ran into the same stubborn secrecy. Adams became convinced that under the superficial layer of their converted Christianity the Samoans preserved a secret priesthood mightier than the po-litical chiefs, with supernatural powers, invocations, proph-ecies, charms, and the whole paraphernalia of paganism. The natives never had to kill a missionary. They merely played him off.

On their *malangas,* or boat excursions, to the smaller is-lands, the two friends thrust themselves deeper and deeper into the Polynesian mystery. How had the natives ever got there? From east or west? Was Darwin correct about the origin of coral reefs? La Farge despaired of duplicating the quality of the light, and Adams of catching the true expres-sion of the islands. To John Hay he wrote that it was languor that was not languid, voluptuousness that was not voluptu-ous, a poem without poetry. At other moments it struck him as simply an impossible stage decoration. Gazing at the natives passing his cottage in their blue or red or yellow waist-cloths, their chocolate shins aglow in the sun against the surf line of the coral reef, he wrote Anna Lodge that he expected to see a prima donna in green garlands and a girdle of ti leaves emerge from the next hut to invoke the cuttlefish or the shark with a Wagnerian chorus of native maidens.

But in the end reality surpassed all such images. Perhaps Adams's most vivid memory would be the picnic by the sliding rock where he watched the yellow limbs of the girls who plunged naked into the white foam, like goldfish in a blue green pool. La Farge said that had they stayed much longer they would have plunged in after them. La Farge, alone, might have.

Before leaving Samoa they became fairly intimate with the Robert Louis Stevensons. The congeniality was more with La Farge than with Adams. The latter was not notably enthusiastic about Stevenson, who put him in mind of a dirty cotton bag over a skeleton. The flashing dark eyes, the darting body, the improbable tales made him uneasy. Adams recoiled from the physical messiness of the Stevensons and may have ascribed some of this quality to Stevenson's mental processes. In this he was certainly unfair. Adams himself had turned away from life in wandering to the Polynesian islands; Stevenson had been searching for it. A condemned asthmatic, he found an additional four years of life in the South Seas. He gave himself fully to the Samoan experience; he dug roots, cut trees, and helped with the building of his house at Vailima like a man on the frontier. He entered passionately into the political disputes of the island and fiercely embraced the side of the natives against that of the exploiting colonials. Adams felt that Stevenson could never understand the Samoans because he ascribed to them the motivations of boys in the Edinburgh of his own youth. But I wonder if Stevenson's understanding of boys and of adventure did not put him closer to the Samoans than Adams could ever have been.

After Samoa came the appalling disillusionment of Tahiti. Adams described it as an exquisitely successful cemetery. The atmosphere was one of hopelessness and premature decay. The natives were not the gay, big animal creatures of Samoa; they were still, silent, sad in expression and fearfully few in number. The population had been decimated by bacteria brought in by westerners. Rum was the only amusement that civilization and religion had left the people. The puppet king, Pomare, was to die of a rotten liver shortly after Adams and La Farge had left. Tahiti was a halfway house between Hawaii and Samoa. Adams complained that a pervasive half castitude permeated everything, a sickly whitish brown or dirty white complexion that suggested weakness and disease.

He was bored, he insisted, as he had never been bored in the worst wilds of Beacon Street or the dreariest dinner tables of Belgravia. While waiting for a boat to take them elsewhere, anywhere, he amused himself by returning to his role of historian and interviewing members of the deposed royal family, the Tevas. Next to Mataafa in Samoa, he found the old ex-queen of Tahiti, Hinari (or Grandmother), the most interesting native figure in the Pacific. She showed none of the secrecy of the Samoan chiefs, but took a motherly interest in Adams and La Farge and told them freely, sitting on the floor, all her clan's oldest legends and traditions. Adams was even adopted into the Teva clan and given the hereditary family name of Taura-Atua with the lands, rights, and privileges attached to it — though those consisted of only a few hundred square feet.

But when he came, some years later, to put it into a book

that he had privately printed, it was little more than an interesting failure. Tahiti had no history, in the western sense of the word, until the arrival of the white man. Of the thousands of years that had preceded Captain Cook, where generation had succeeded generation without distinguishable change, there was nothing left but genealogy and legend. The genealogy, which makes up a large part of Adams's book, is boring, and, as for the legend, he himself admitted that he needed the lighter hand of Stevenson.

Yet *The Memoirs of Arii Taimai* nonetheless marks an important step in Adams's career. He had gone, by 1890, as far as he was going as a historian in the conventional sense. His great work on Jefferson and Madison was history at its most intellectually pure. The author stands aside and lets the documents tell the story, from which a very few precious rules may be deduced. But in the South Seas he had tried to leave the intellect for simplicity, for instinct. He had sought peace and found ennui. Even the unspoiled natives, in the long run, palled. He had to return, in Papeete, to his profession, and he had to try it with a new twist, for how else could Tahitian history be done? And if *The Memoirs* were a bore, was it altogether his fault? Might it not be in the subject? Suppose he were to happen upon a subject that required not only the imagination of the man who had sat on the floor with the old queen of Tahiti as she intoned the poems of her family tradition, but also the industry of the devoted scholar who had pored through archives of European foreign offices? Suppose he were to find a subject, in short, that required a great artist as well as a great historian?

He was to find such a one a few years hence in the Gothic cathedrals of France. *Mont-St. Michel and Chartres* is an extraordinary tour de force of the imagination, a vivid invocation of the spirit and force of the twelfth century that may be longer read than any of Adams's other books. It has always been a difficult volume for librarians to classify. Is it history or travel or criticism or theology or even fiction? But its language shimmers with some of the magic blue of the windows of the cathedral that forms its principal topic. One day, at the Metropolitan Museum of Art, gazing at the brilliant *Ia Orana Maria*, I was struck by the fact that the Virgin of Chartres, like the Virgin of Paul Gauguin, may owe something to the colors and legends of the South Seas.

Gauguin arrived in Tahiti a few days after Adams and La Farge had left, in time to witness the funeral of King Pomare. It is probably just as well that they did not meet. The American travelers detested European settlers, and a European settler who drank to excess and lived publicly with a native woman would have seemed the acme of western corruption. If Adams had considered Stevenson a bohemian, Gauguin would have been beyond the pale. Nor would La Farge have liked Gauguin's painting. Many years later, when he and Adams were old men and Gauguin was dead, La Farge wrote to his former traveling companion about an illustrated catalogue of a Gauguin show in Paris. He informed Adams that the "mad Frenchman" had been in Tahiti shortly after their visit and had actually met some of their friends. It is disappointing to have to relate that he went on to say that Gauguin's paintings were sorry failures, desperate efforts to catch the attention of a novelty-hunting public.

It has been said that Gauguin, with his brilliant colors and primitive figures, caught the essential atmosphere of the islands that both Adams and La Farge missed. But what he really did was to create a Polynesia of his own that millions of his admirers now regard as the true one. Gauguin came to

Tahiti naively in search of an island paradise, an unspoiled Arcadia, but he found and recognized in Papeete precisely what Adams had found and recognized. Only on canvas could he realize his dream.

He was under no illusions about what he was doing. His red seas and blue dogs were perfectly deliberate. He wanted painting to stand independent of what it purported to represent and not to be a branch of sculpture. He said that the kind of people who desired exact reproduction would have to wait for the invention of a color camera. They have, and they are quite content!

Of the brilliant four who were in the Polynesian islands in 1891: Adams, Stevenson, Gauguin, and La Farge, the first three, like most artists, brought more with them than they were to take out. The subjective experiences of the historian, of the storyteller and of the post-Impressionist might have been much the same in other parts of the globe. Polynesia simply happened to be the stage of one aspect of their development. But in La Farge I feel a more objective effort to reproduce the islands.

His stubborn imagination fixed them in a classic atmosphere that seemed proof against disillusionment. To him the blues and greens were painted in lines of Homer, guessed at by Titian, and the long sway and cadence of the surf had the music of the Odyssey. The Samoan youngster with a red hibiscus fastened in his hair by a grassy knot was a Bacchus of Tintoretto. La Farge prided himself on having an affinity with a remoter ancestry of man and on being better able than other westerners to understand the islanders.

But if his paintings have a charm that may be special and Polynesian, they are still romantic. They still tell us quite as much of John La Farge as they do of Samoa. Perhaps it is because he insisted the paradise that Gauguin knew was dead still existed. And perhaps this very insistence is the one good thing that came out of the meeting of east and west. The dream of innocence, abided in or awoken from, may yet be a mighty source of inspiration.

Lytton Strachey:
The Last Elizabethan

THE REPUTATION OF Lytton Strachey has had its ups and downs. In his own day he was considered by many to be too cynical, too willing to sacrifice a dull truth to an amusing gibe. A later generation accused him less of unkindness than of superficiality, and more recently there have been those who profess to see in his portraits of nineteenth-century characters more sentimentality than irreverence. That he should have ever been regarded as a debunker of Queen Victoria and General Gordon, these maintain, is simply evidence of how besotted his first readers still were with Victorian folklore. Why, he adored the grumpy old queen!

Yet even conceding some portion of truth to each of these points of view, I am still of the opinion that his three masterpieces, *Eminent Victorians, Queen Victoria,* and *Elizabeth and Essex,* deserve to stand as highly as when they first appeared in 1918, 1921, and 1928, respectively.

In the cases of three famous English women, Victoria, Elizabeth I, and Florence Nightingale, Strachey's portraits have become the accepted, the so-to-speak National Portrait Gallery ones, and this despite the subsequent release of huge

masses of documentation not available in his lifetime. Cecil
Woodham-Smith's biography of Miss Nightingale (published
in 1951 as *Lonely Crusader*) fills in every wrinkle of the subject's countenance, but the general outline is still Strachey's.
Similarly it is Strachey's conception of the Virgin Queen that
has become the traditional one on the stage and in historical
fiction despite shelves of other studies, showing her as everything from a mere tool of Burleigh to a sovereign who owed
all her success to luck.

The release of Queen Victoria's official correspondence,
after the biography had appeared, showed a sovereign more
insistent on imagined royal prerogatives and more of a
headache to her ministers than Strachey had envisioned, but
here again the principal characteristics of his queen endure.
His two Victorias, the young and old, are the ones of whom
we are most conscious today: the sober, methodical little
princess who wanted to be good, the "small, smooth crystal
pebble, without a flaw and without a scintillation," and the
venerable ruler of Kipling's " 'alf of creation," the very sym-
bol of England's extraordinary and mysterious destiny.
Strachey was able to convey to the reading public Victoria's
peculiar fascination: her directness, her literalness, her stubbornness, her delight in the exotic and the charlatan, her
total lack of discrimination, her terrible rigidity, her ultimately pathetic efforts to defeat time by preserving everything: letters, pictures, statues, bibelots in vast, cluttered,
never-changing rooms and by freezing the days and nights
into a remorseless, quaintly middle-class etiquette.

What is more remarkable even than his comprehension of
these women is his insight into their respective eras: into
the demonic earnestness and childlike naiveté of the Victorian age and into the golden blend of idealism and cruelty

that was an integral part of the English Renaissance. Indeed, the essence of his art is the ability to delineate an era through its representative citizens.

At first glance his eminent Victorians — a cardinal, a nurse, a headmaster, and a soldier — might seem to have little in common, but as the book unfolds we appreciate the common denominator of Cardinal Manning's literal interpretation of the early Christian fathers, Florence Nightingale's ingenuous proof of the existence of God, Dr. Arnold's delight in the society of the "good poor," and General Gordon's habit of adding the initials d.v. (*deo volente*) to every statement of futurity. One wonders if there was ever an age when man regarded himself as more the center of the universe.

But to my mind Strachey's peculiar genius was in understanding the age of Elizabeth. There man's position was regarded as more precarious. He might have been "the beauty of the world, the paragon of animals," but he was also the "quintessence of dust." Strachey's tour de force in *Elizabeth and Essex* was to present his "tragic history" in terms of Elizabethan drama. Essex, the protagonist, is a man of the Renaissance, wayward, melancholy, splendid, but he is also the last fine flower of feudalism, "radiant with the colors of antique knighthood" and doomed in conflict with the cool, dry-eyed servants of absolutism, the Bacons and Cecils, in whom the crafty old queen, however in love with chivalry, placed her ultimate reliance. It is a book, like the contemporary tragedies of blood, full of terrible, magnificent deaths: Essex stretching out his scarlet-sleeved arms as the signal for his own execution, Philip of Spain waiting in his great dark tomb of a palace to be welcomed into heaven by the Trinity, old Gloriana lying speechless on a cushioned floor, four days and four nights, with her finger in her mouth. I confess to finding little exaggeration in Max Beerbohm's judgment that for "sheer divine beauty of prose" nobody came within a hundred miles of Strachey.

The strong colors, the vividness, the passions of the era appealed to Strachey and to his literary friends of Bloomsbury. Their own world seemed drabber to them, duller, less congenial to romance and legend. As Virginia Woolf wrote in *Orlando:*

The age was Elizabethan; their morals were not ours; nor their poets; nor their climate; nor their vegetables even. Everything was different. The weather itself, the heat and cold of summer and winter, was, we may believe, of another temper altogether. The brilliant amorous day was divided as sheerly from the night as land from water. Sunsets were redder and more intense; dawns were whiter and more amoral. Of our crepuscular half-lights and lingering twilights they knew nothing.

But if the "brilliant amorous day" was divided so sheerly from the night, there was no such sharp demarcation between the sexes. Strachey was charmed by this ambivalence: the sumptuous vestments, the jewels, the earrings, of the beautiful, strutting Essex and the passionate temper and domineering attitudes of the old queen. Essex could take to his bed for days at a time in fits of melancholy; he could sigh and weep; he was moody, petulant, and childish, while Elizabeth was capable of sending men and women to torture and death without a qualm. On the other side, Essex was gallant in battle, quick to make love to court beauties and to fight duels with rivals, while the queen, by the standards of her day, was nothing if not feminine in her jealousy, her vanity, and her procrastination. It was as if each had the qualities of both sexes, like those heroines of Shakespeare who appear to such advantage in male attire.

Strachey presents his book almost as a stage tragedy. The characters are so carefully delineated that when at last they are suddenly quoted, in letters or despatches or reported sayings, they come startlingly to life. We seem to hear Elizabeth when she retorts to the Polish envoy in angry Latin, or Essex when he claps his hand to his sword in the queen's very presence, and shouts that she has outraged him. We might be at the Globe and Essex a Hamlet, ruminating, vengeful, passionate; Bacon, an aristocratic Iago and Robert Cecil a cool Octavius. And Elizabeth? Well, there is no character in all of Elizabethan drama like its namesake, but she is of its essence.

Saint-Simon:
Novelist or Historian?

THE TRIUMPH OF THE writer over his contemporaries, which Shakespeare celebrated in his sonnets, warning his patron, the Earl of Southampton, that the latter's immortality would depend on the poor poet's rhyme, is nowhere more dramatically illustrated than in the voluminous memoirs of the Duc de Saint-Simon. For the whole glittering pageant of the court of Louis XIV, the wonder of its world, survives to us only because it was minutely described by a man who despised its creator. It is as if the White House under Harry Truman survived in the journals of General MacArthur, or Woodrow Wilson in the tender memories of Henry Cabot Lodge.

Now, of course, it is true that the very court the angry little duke so gloriously describes was devised by the monarch as a means of keeping the once powerful and troublemaking peers of France occupied with innocuous duties and diversions. Versailles was a machine that turned potential *frondeurs* into puppets in periwigs who danced attendance on the royal family. And nobody fell more deeply into the nets of etiquette and precedence than Saint-Simon himself.

It was not a question of missing the substance behind the forms. He believed the forms to *be* the substance. He hated Louis XIV for catching all the titled fish of France without ever realizing how greedily he himself had gobbled the bait.

Saint-Simon sought to reestablish the power of the nobles by playing the game of etiquette even more intensely than Louis XIV meant it to be played. The privileges of handing a shirt or a chamber pot to a prince, or of remaining covered in his presence, or of being seated on a tabouret, were the objects of his buzzing, busy life. By the sheer brilliance of his artistry as a diarist he made the artificial world of the court seem the real world. His final revenge on a world that gave him status without power was to paint it as a world that cared only for status.

The last episode of the memoirs, the trip to Madrid, seems an argument for those who would classify the little duke as a novelist rather than a historian. It provides the climax to which the earlier volumes build: the apotheosis of Saint-Simon as Ambassador Extraordinary to the Court of Spain on the purely formal business of signing a royal marriage contract. To be sure, the contract was an important one. It embraced not only the proposed union of the young Louis XV with the Infanta Maria-Anna, but that of the French regent's daughter with the heir to the Spanish throne. But what one is apt to forget in reading Saint-Simon's absorbing account is that the terms had all been agreed upon before he was appointed.

He uses a good, classic plot. The ambassador sets forth on his odyssey to perform a task that seems impossible. A cabal in the regent's court, determined to make the mission the duke's ruin, has spiked his instructions with demands for precedence that the Spanish court cannot possibly grant, and it has saddled him with an entourage designed to bring him to bankruptcy. In Madrid more problems loom. Should the king sign the contract by his own hand or by proxy? Should there be witnesses, and if so should they be French or Spanish? How many copies should be signed? Should the papal nuncio execute the contract before the French ambassador?

Saint-Simon, a d'Artagnan of ceremonial, triumphs over every ambush, slipping in between the king and nuncio under the pretense of being overwhelmed by the greatness of the occasion and seizing the pen, as in a trance, before the pope's representative can get his hand on it. Victory comes at last with the dispatch from Paris that the regent's daughter, Mademoiselle de Montpensier, is actually on her way, and Saint-Simon hastens at night with flickering torches to the palace to be admitted to the very bedroom of their Catholic Majesties with his great news!

So far the novel. But Mademoiselle de Montpensier, aged twelve, sullen little pawn of diplomats, a princess torn from home and mother to be married in a strange land to a child prince, brings history with her. She has her revenge on her father through his Ambassador Extraordinary in the only way she knows. When Saint-Simon comes to take his official leave, his mission completed, before departing for Paris, he finds her standing on a dais, her ladies on one side, the grandees on another. He makes three deep reverences, utters his compliments, but receives no answer.

After some moments of silence, I asked her what messages she had for the King, or for her parents, or grandmother. In reply she simply stared at me, and then suddenly belched in my face so loudly that it echoed through the chamber. I was stupefied. A second belch followed, as noisy as the first, whereupon I lost control and burst out laughing. A third belch, still louder than the other two, threw everyone into confusion and forced me to take ignominious flight, followed by all my suite, amid shrieks of laughter.

I do not wish to suggest that poor little Mademoiselle de Montpensier's protest is a fitting commentary on Saint-Simon's great work. But it is good every now and then, under the spell of his pages, to be reminded that the bulk of humanity, then as now, cared little for his preoccupations. It is healthy to recall that his great mission to Madrid was a mere formality, the cabal against him probably imaginary, and their Catholic Majesties bored to tears by his compliments. Their ennui, however, becomes our ultimate amusement. The family of Philip V entertains posterity through the little duke as their descendants entertain it through Goya. The artist (or is it the historian?) has the last laugh.

The Clergy of Barchester

ANTHONY TROLLOPE is the despair of academe: no symbols, no layers of meaning, no subtlety as to points of view, no proper respect, in short, for the craft of fiction. Pre–Henry James and hence literarily unbaptized, he must be relegated to a purgatory of the unprivileged but well-meaning. Indeed, was he even well-meaning? Did he not relegate himself rather to the hell of the Philistines by boasting that he wrote for money and by keeping office hours for fiction, starting a new novel on the very day he finished the old? Did he not lard his books with hunting scenes simply because he loved the sport and take his readers into his confidence in clumsy Thackerayan "asides" that only Thackeray could handle? Did he not hurry home after overhearing two men at his club complain that they were bored with Mrs. Proudie, and kill her off in the current work? Could one imagine James so butchering Aunt Maud in *The Wings of the Dove?*

James himself had initially no great opinion of Trollope. Of an Atlantic crossing in 1876 he wrote to his family:

We had also Anthony Trollope who wrote novels in his state-room (he does it literally every morning in his life, no matter where he may be) and played cards with Mrs. Bronson all the evening. He has a gross and repulsive face and manner, but appears *bon enfant* when you talk with him.

But when Trollope died six years later, James wrote a moving essay of appreciation. While admitting that Trollope had no system, doctrine, or form and that he might even have thought it dangerous to be too explicitly or consciously an artist, he lauded him for his knowledge of people:

Trollope's great apprehension of the real, which was what made him so interesting, came to him through his desire to satisfy us on this point — to tell us what certain people were and what they did in consequence of being so. That is the purpose of each of his tales; and if these things produce an illusion it comes from the gradual abundance of his testimony as to the temper, the tone, the passions, the habits, the moral nature, of a certain number of contemporary Britons.

There may be in reading Trollope some of the fascination of watching an electric train in a toy store window darting down a track by the stations and plastic hotels, turning at little signals, whizzing into tunnels and past miniature cars halted at grade crossings. I remember going to a lecture on Trollope's characters at the Grolier Club in New York and hearing the elderly fanatics afterward discussing Lady Glen and Planty Pall as if they were personal friends. Trollopians love to draw maps of Allington and Barchester and the cathedral close and to argue whether Lily Dale should have married Johnny Eames and what would have happened to the bishop's domestic rebellion had Mrs. Proudie not conveniently died.

But what is all this but a tribute to Trollope the observer? Like Sinclair Lewis in a later era, he was the master journalist among the fiction writers of his day. In his job of inspecting postal routes in England and Ireland he explored those countries as no other novelist ever has. In a lifetime that embraced poverty and affluence, a successful career in government as well as letters, travels abroad to Africa, North America, and Australia, Trollope equipped himself uniquely to paint the portrait of mid-Victorian England. He knew peers, politicians, artists, lawyers, clergymen, tradesmen, farmers, and clerks, and he had the fertile imagination to re-create them in a library of fiction considered huge even in that prolific age. I should not be distressed to hear that *Jane Eyre* or *Wuthering Heights* contained unrecognizable pictures of Yorkshire in the 1840s, for I read those novels for other merits. But if I were told that Trollope had seriously misrepresented the clergy of Barchester I would shut up his books at once.

That is not to say that, bathed in his own time, he was free from its prejudices. Far from it. Any constant reader of Trollope (and there is so much of him and most of it is of so consistently high a level of entertainment that reading him can become a drug) will from time to time be repelled by an overexposure to mid-Victorian complacency. It is all very well for his defenders to point out individual examples of Trollopian broadmindedness. I concede that a fallen woman is an object of sympathy in *The Vicar of Bullhampton,* and that the heroine of *Lady Anna* marries a tailor. But throughout the bulk of his fiction Trollope makes it perfectly clear that his heroes are gentlemen and his heroines ladies, that they confine themselves quite properly to their own kind, and that any man who sneers at good English institutions such as titles, country estates, horse racing, and fox hunting is apt to be a bit of a cad. His villains, indeed, are usually nonathletic.

Trollope may have appeared liberal to some readers in his

belief in a basic equality within the class defined as "gentle-men." He did not think, for example, that the daughter of a duke demeaned herself in marrying a country squire, pro-vided the latter was a good fellow and understood the role of dukes in the British establishment. But this democracy was confined to the upper and upper-middle classes. A good girl, like Eleanor Bold in *Barchester Towers,* is cut to the quick by the mere suspicion in her family that she may be planning to marry Obadiah Slope. And Henry Grantly pulls his father up sharply when the latter suggests that he has be-come attached to a young woman living in Silverbridge:

Is there any reason why I should not become attached to a young woman in Silverbridge? — though I hope any young woman to whom I may become attached will be worthy at any rate of being called a young lady.

To which the archdeacon responds fervently: "I hope so, Henry; I hope so. I do hope so."

But these impressions, as I have said, come from an *over-dose* of Trollope. In the same way one may be fatigued by his repetitiousness and the flat quality of his eternal common sense. As in Molière, too much of that virtue can be repel-lent. In each novel, however, judged by itself, there is enough restraint and fairness on the author's part to enable the reader to adjust his sights and view what I take to be a fairly accurate panorama of mid-Victorian manners. I am con-vinced, for example, perhaps arbitrarily, that Trollope's glorious lawyers, with their admirable powers of deduction, are absolutely true to life. I am aware that his peers are sometimes said to be poorly drawn, but peers are always said to be poorly drawn by those who profess to know them, and I still believe in the De Courcys and the Pallisers. And when we come to his clerics — well, if *they* are wrong, then fiction is greater than fact, for they have crept into history to take the places of their models.

Trollope's reputation took a notorious dip after his death in 1882 and the publication of his autobiography. The latter was too candid and too pedestrian to Victorian readers who liked to think of their favorites as "inspired." But in the present times, and particularly during the Second World War, he has come again into popularity, because, it is sometimes argued, his world seems safe and idyllic in contrast to our own. I think it is more than that. I think it is because the Trollopian world was confined. It had, so to speak, a top, a bottom, and sides, whereas we have lived since 1939 in space, politically, morally, and physically. Nothing today, alas, is inconceivable, even for the Duke of Omnium's son to marry a kitchen maid, even for the population of the globe to be obliterated. English society, as Trollope saw it, was a more or less orderly but flexible hierarchy where a man of education had a perfectly decent chance to ascend the social ladder, without becoming a crook or a sycophant, so long as he didn't upset the persons in power with too many radical or wild ideas. He himself had worked his way from poverty to relative affluence in the civil service and, ultimately, through his novels, to something like wealth. For all the misery of his childhood, for all the arrogance and even corruption that he viewed in high places, he did not find England a bad place in which to live.

The Church of England was the microcosm through which he most penetratingly described his nation. The series known as the Barchester novels includes *The Warden, Barchester Towers, Doctor Thorne, Framley Parsonage, The Small House at Allington,* and *The Last Chronicle of Barset. Doctor Thorne* and *The Small House at Allington* are not herein considered as they do not deal with the clergy of Barchester. The other four, taken together, comprise a lively and cohesive treatise on the antiquated but by no means moribund British religious system in an era of vigorous reform.

The Warden presents us right off with a characteristic problem: a hospital for a handful of old men, created under an ancient will, is administered by a saintly cleric, Septimus Harding, who is in no way responsible for the ludicrous disproportion between his handsome salary and his almost nonexistent duties. But there it is, a sinecure, and when John Bold triggers off a newspaper campaign against it, the poor warden is held up to savage ridicule and contempt. The tempest is the lens through which Trollope views what is happening in the Church.

The bishop of Barchester and Archdeacon Grantly represent the establishment. They stand on the record and use without scruple every procedural trick their reputable counsel can devise to avoid a trial on the merits. What is right, to the archdeacon, is simply what the church is and has. It cannot give up one jot or one tittle without a dangerous loss of face. John Bold and the newspapers berate them unmercifully, firm in their faith that this sinecure is but one of many offenses and that violence alone will reform the establishment. Septimus Harding, crushed between prosecution and defense, resigns his wardenship, preferring poverty to an uneasy conscience.

The book is a masterpiece of fairness. Trollope might have made as good a lawyer as one of his fictional solicitors. It is perfectly evident that he dislikes the character assassinations of the newspapers and the reforming zeal of John Bold, but a radical could not have made a better case for them. It is also evident that he has a partiality for the worldly archdeacon, but he bears down with gleeful emphasis on his vanity and pompousness. Grantly is known to the old men at the hospital as "Calves" in reference to the splendor of his "nether regions." He can see no reason that his late father, the bishop, should not have reaped a fortune in the days when it was "worth a man's while to be Bishop of Barchester." In return for his own emoluments it is quite enough if he supports the church with his presence, his eloquence, and his studied magnificence.

Yet his father-in-law, the warden, is just the reverse, a kind, godly man, humble to the point of meekness, yet capable of being firm as granite where a moral principle is involved. Trollope seems to be telling us that the church, like every other Victorian institution, is a mixture of good and bad, but that the good, like the British army, can be counted on to win the last battle.

He seems less sure of this, however, in the next novel. *Barchester Towers* may not be the greatest of Trollope's novels — it lacks the high seriousness of *The Last Chronicle* and the impressive anger of *The Way We Live Now* — but, as Hugh Walpole said of it, it is the most "Trollopian." If one does not like *Barchester Towers,* one had better turn away from Trollope. It is again a dramatization of the struggle for power among the clergy of the diocese of Barchester: very funny, very shrewd, and at times a bit appalling. Trollope, like so many nineteenth-century authors, was fascinated by power: in the church, in government, in county life, and he was able to make his contests at least seem evenly balanced.

The principal struggle in *Barchester Towers* is between Mrs. Proudie, the bishop's wife, and Obadiah Slope, his chaplain, as to which shall be the real bishop. It is made more interesting by the fact that, in its initial stages, only Slope is aware of it. Mrs. Proudie believes that he is her ally and has no suspicion that she is being undermined. She has everything on her side, or seems to have. She rules Barchester like a despotic Tudor queen, not bothering to make her commands palatable, relishing the cringing with which her almost unbelievable rudeness is met. There have been readers who have found Mrs. Proudie overdrawn. But surely to those of us raised on American cartoons of the American dowager, there is nothing extraordinary about the domination of an ugly, humorless, dogmatic, and egotistical female by sheer strength of will. Mrs. Proudie rules her household by the simple expedient of making life intolerable for rebels. She is almost sympathetic in the totality of her outrageousness.

Obadiah Slope, to match himself against this virago, has to be what his creator calls "a bit of a genius." Not only does he aim to control the bishop; he means to substitute Mr. Harding for Mrs. Proudie's candidate as warden of Hiram's Hospital, marry Mr. Harding's rich widowed daughter, and raise himself to the deanship of Barchester. It is a mad scheme for a man as unlovely and as unlovable as Slope, but he has on his side an unscrupulousness as perfect as Mrs. Proudie's outrageousness. His professed religious convictions (for the moment, low church), his sermons, and his promises are mere tools in the job of self-aggrandizement.

Sheila Kaye-Smith, writing of *Pride and Prejudice,* defended Lady Catherine de Bourgh and Mr. Collins from the charge of being caricatures in a novel of real characters by comparing them to a pair of Toby jugs on a shelf of Dresden china. "They do not really belong, but they look fine." The same might be said of Mrs. Proudie and Slope. And yet, when Trollope came to kill Mrs. Proudie in *The Last Chronicle of Barset,* she dies convincingly, despite the tradition that comic characters are immortal. Standing up by her bed in sudden death, mortally frustrated by Crawley's defiance and by her worm of a husband's final turning, she is at last a pathetic, if not a tragic figure.

The Signora Neroni, penniless, crippled, disreputable, unscrupulous and utterly charming, succeeds at last in getting Slope in trouble with Mrs. Proudie, but this is not what brings his plans to ultimate ruin. Trollope devised an elaborate plot to trace the battle between Mrs. Proudie and her rebellious chaplain, but at the climax he is too honest not to admit that this battle has been illusory. Mrs. Proudie has only to be alone once with her husband to annihilate Slope. It is too bad that her victory should be so simple after all his desperate stratagems, but that is the way of the world. Slope never really has a chance, either to defeat Mrs. Proudie, or to marry Eleanor Bold, or to become dean of Barchester. Nor have we ever been allowed to believe that he would. Our suspense has been created entirely over each rung; we always know that the ladder will ultimately topple on him.

I am a bit sorry for Obadiah Slope. He is stepped on as if he were a bug, and I do not altogether like Eleanor Bold for being insulted at the mere suggestion that she might marry him. But there I get back to the Victorian complacency of Trollope. Love is an attraction between ladies and gentlemen. Some of his romances tumble out of the novels as if they were old valentines stuck in as bookmarks by his contemporary readers. The Trollope we like today is the creator of Slope and Mrs. Proudie, not of Eleanor Bold and Arabin. The miasma of sentimentality that clouded the Victorian era affected Trollope quite as much as it did his adored Thackeray. Where we relish them both today is where they break through it. I doubt if the time will ever come when readers of *Vanity Fair* will prefer Amelia Sedley to Becky Sharp.

There is happily no sentimentality about the Stanhope family in *Barchester Towers*. The Reverend Vesey Stanhope enjoys a clerical sinecure that makes Mr. Harding's at Hiram's Hospital seem like hard work. This elegant younger brother of a peer and his decorous, indolent family have been living for ten years in Italy on revenues drawn entirely from the livings of Barchester. They are sincerely outraged when Bishop Proudie requests that Vesey Stanhope spend a little time in the diocese and look languidly about Barchester to see what it has to offer them. It has nothing but Eleanor Bold's fortune, and Bertie Stanhope is too languid even to get that. Their only fleeting triumph is the Signora Neroni's at Mrs. Proudie's reception, when a caster of her sofa does horrendous damage to her hostess' gown. But thereafter the Stanhopes fade, and I suspect Trollope tired of them. Their interest lies in their situation, and when this has been described, what are they? Even the Signora becomes prosy and dull. It is inconceivable that the charmer of the early chapters could have become the speechifier of the later. And in the end, where she tells Arabin to press his suit to Eleanor, thus giving herself the glory of one disinterested act, she is a pale echo of Becky Sharp telling Amelia about George Osborne. When Trollope copied Thackeray, he always did it badly.

Trollope considered *The Last Chronicle of Barset* his greatest novel, and I agree with his choice. Of course, he was thinking of that portion of it that deals with the indictment of the Reverend Josiah Crawley, "perpetual curate" of Hogglestock, for the theft of a twenty-pound note. The subsidiary plots of Grace Crawley's romance with Henry Grantly and John Eames' involvement with a gang of loan sharks are good standard Trollope, but with Crawley he at last reaches the heights of Thackeray in *The Newcomes*.

The situation is simple. Crawley has endorsed and cashed a twenty-pound check drawn to bearer by an estate agent who maintains that he never gave it to Crawley but might have dropped it by error in his house. Crawley cannot recall how he got possession of the check and offers conflicting stories. To the scandalization of Barsetshire, he is indicted. Some believe him innocent; some, guilty; some, insane. He has always stood apart from the ecclesiastical establishment, poor but intensely proud, a scholar, an ascetic (in all but matrimony), fanatically devoted to his clerical duties, a man whose only diversion is reading ancient authors and whose only expressed desire is to visit the Holy Land. What a satisfaction to the fat cats in surplices if this tortured, righteous priest, whose very existence is a reproach to them, should turn out to be a hypocrite!

Of course, he turns out to be nothing of the sort. Possession of the check was innocently gained. Crawley is too unworldly to have taken proper care of such matters. But the real fire to which the accused man is subjected is not so much his humiliation in the eyes of a world that he scorns as in the light cast into his own soul. Crawley can shout "Peace, woman!" to the terrible Mrs. Proudie when she interrupts his conference with the bishop — yes, and silence her, too — but he is less assured when he begins to suspect that the sin of pride is in his own heart.

At first there is a kind of dusky exaltation in his downfall. Summoned to the bishop's palace he insists on going by foot, and his thoughts are as fierce as those of John the Baptist before Herod:

He took great glory from the thought that he would go before the bishop with dirty boots — with boots necessarily dirty — with rusty pantaloons, that he would be hot and mud-stained with his walk, hungry, and an object to be wondered at by all who should see him, because of the misfortunes which had been unworthily heaped upon his head, whereas the bishop would be sleek and clean and well-fed — pretty with all the prettinesses that are becoming to a bishop's outward man . . . And yet he would take the bishop in his grasp and crush him — crush him — crush him!

Nowhere in Trollope is the power of one man so felt as in the Crawley chapters. And yet, if Crawley can subdue those about him, he cannot subdue his own growing doubts about himself. He begins to see that it "was not sufficient for him to remember that he knew Hebrew, but he must remember also that the dean did not." King Lear on the heath admits his faults only in general terms; he is incapable of recognizing that he has behaved pettishly. But Crawley undergoes the more painful and humbling experience of confronting his own egotism. If ever there was a man who pierced to the heart of his own character, even into the deepest cell of his own vanity, it is this would-be martyr whose conscience will ultimately deny his diet even the bare bone of self-pity.

The fineness with which he is drawn makes the chapters in which he does not appear seem longer than they would in a more typically Trollopian novel. In a recent rereading of *The Last Chronicle* I learned why it had been so easy for the BBC to translate the Parliamentary novels into a popular television serial. The dialogue is not only brilliant, it is self-sufficient. Try reading one of the novels in dialogue alone and see how much is missed. Indeed, something may even be gained, for Trollope had a habit of repeating himself, so that some of his descriptive passages recall the style of the children's writer, Thornton W. Burgess, who used to tell us: "Peter Rabbit was scared. Yes, sir, Peter Rabbit was scared. Peter Rabbit was scared as he had never been scared before. Peter Rabbit was scared of Farmer Brown's boy . . ."

Crawley does something else by contrast to the rest of the

novel. He dates it. Because he is seen in depth it does not matter that he is a man of habits and beliefs alien to our own times. He is true. But when his daughter Grace insists that she will not marry Henry Grantly unless her father be acquitted — and this despite her absolute confidence in his innocence — she is paying a tribute to the power of public opinion that shows her to be simply morally fashionable. And when Lily Dale vows herself to a life of celibacy because of her betrayal by Crosbie, turning down honest Johnny Eames, we think her a fool. Did Trollope? No. He allows us to express our own feelings through his more worldly, realistic characters, but he reserves his own highest admiration for heroines true to the Victorian image. Happily, the portrait of Crawley took him to deeper values.

With Crawley and with Septimus Harding, the warden, the moral account of the Church of England seems to be almost in the black. What of the villains? Obadiah Slope is about as low as they get, although he at least performs his duties, unlike Bishop Proudie, who surrenders his miter to his wife, and Vesey Stanhope, who lives in Italy. From Harding to Slope, then: that is the moral range of the church as Trollope sees it. Perhaps it averages out in Mark Robarts, the clergyman hero of *Framley Parsonage*. Robarts is a handsome, easy-going, smart young man who, because of his college friendship with Lord Lufton, is given the excellent living that Lord Lufton controls. This is obviously not fair to other young ministers who are less fortunate in their social connections. On the other hand, considering what the system is, the parishioners are lucky to get as good a man as Robarts, who is obviously going somewhere in the church. Robarts has a curate for his chores, a carriage for his family, and a footman for his table. He can afford to spend weekends with the local gentry and even to hunt. He gets into bad company, signs his name as accommodation to a gambler's note, and is in trouble. But one feels in the end, when Lord Lufton rescues him, that he has learned his lesson. If Robarts ever becomes a bishop, he will be no Proudie.

Trollope was to go on to other fields of English life, but he never did better than with the clergy. As James put it:

What he had picked up, to begin with, was a comprehensive, various impression of the clergy of the Church of England and the manners and feelings that prevail in cathedral towns. This, for a while, was his specialty, and, as always happens in such cases, the public was disposed to prescribe to him that path. He knew about bishops, archdeacons, prebendaries, precentors, and about their wives and daughters; he knew what these dignitaries say to each other when they are collected together, aloof from secular ears. He even knew what sort of talk goes on between a bishop and a bishop's lady when the august couple are enshrouded in the privacy of the episcopal bedroom. This knowledge, somehow, was rare and precious. No one, as yet, had been bold enough to snatch the illuminating torch from the very summit of the altar.

Rebecca West in *The Court and the Castle* has suggested that Trollope's clergymen, like his Parliamentarians, are really civil servants (like Trollope himself) in disguise. But I wonder if there was that much difference between civil servants and the clerics of an established church. Miss West goes on to say that nowhere does Trollope show the kind of biblical or theological scholar that existed in such profusion among the Victorian clergy. It seems to me that she forgets Mr. Crawley. But the point that I see behind her point is that she is offering to defend the Victorian clergy from Trollope's likening of them to bureaucrats, not on the ground of their spirituality but on the ground of their learning. If Trollope's picture be true, except for the aspect of scholarship, the English clergy must have offered little consolation to the parishioner who needed individual help and guidance.

Can anyone imagine discussing a loss of faith with Mark Robarts? Or a sin of the flesh with Bishop Proudie? Or an erring child with Archdeacon Grantly? Even the conscientious priests would be of little help. Harding is too naive; Crawley, too self-absorbed. At worst the clergy is venal; at best it is mystic. Where, outside of the splendid ceremonial, is there help for the troubled soul?

What Trollope understood more keenly and delineated more graphically than any of his contemporaries was the power of human perversity, the stubbornness and self-pity that operate to put things wrong between relatives and friends which could otherwise be easily adjusted. The novels are full of sons determined to be disinherited, of husbands insisting on being jealous, of lovers resolved to be misunderstood. In all of this sparring for defeat the clergy never fall behind. They are in it up to the neck.

Thackeray's "Struggling Genius"

WHEN WILLIAM MAKEPEACE THACKERAY delivered one of his "Four Georges" lectures in Washington in the early winter of 1853, there were two presidents in the audience, Millard Fillmore and Franklin Pierce. The latter was the President-elect, and he entered the hall, according to the elated lecturer, arm in arm with the incumbent. Can one imagine such attention from such quarters being bestowed on any foreign (or even native) novelist today?

Thackeray's popularity, on both sides of the Atlantic, was second only to Dickens's. Perhaps with the upper and upper-middle classes it was even greater. As editor of the widely read *Cornhill Magazine* he was a principal arbiter of British literary taste. It was inevitable that his reputation should have suffered with the reaction to his era in our own century, and it remains a question to this day how much of it can be restored.

For he is still the Victorian of Victorians. He trembled with patriotic emotion at the prospect of the far-flung empire; he rated an English gentleman the finest creation of western civilization; and he reverenced that gentleman's wife if she was chaste and obedient. He reveled in the vast, sooty pile of London with its great mansions and its pomp, its splendid dinner parties and congenial clubs. The tears that he shed over the poor and benighted were sincere but perfunctory; fundamentally, he believed that the establishment was doing as good a job as could be expected. When he wrote of the underprivileged, he emphasized the comic side of their simple ways, particularly as manifested in their grammar and accent. The Jews in his novels are always beak-nosed and money-grubbing, and the blacks are shiftless, happy-go-lucky, and dishonest — except when they forget their station and become sinister. Traveling in the American ante-bellum South he found the slaves well treated and happy. His heart was full of love for his fellow man, but it was not the kind of love that made him wish to rock boats.

His tastes were also those of his time. He rhapsodized to his friend Tennyson over the beauties of *The Idylls of the King;* he enjoyed academic paintings of bloody historical events; he walked out of *La Dame aux Camelias* because it shocked him; and he condemned *Madame Bovary* as "a heartless, cold-blooded study of the downfall and degradation of a woman." Even Mrs. Browning did not escape his censorship at the *Cornhill;* he banned "Lord Walter's Wife," which seems to us the quintessence of nineteenth-century morality, because it dealt with a wife's novel way of handling an improper proposition by her husband's friend. And for all Thackeray's Francophilia and annual visits to Paris, he never made an intimate friend there because he could never quite approve of a Frenchman's morals.

Did Thackeray consider himself a Victorian? Certainly not. No true Victorian ever did. He liked to consider himself an eighteenth-century spirit restrained by prudish customs from telling the truth about a man. I believe that he may have also regarded his tendency to depressions as uncharacteristic of the crude industrial times to which destiny had assigned him. We today, on the contrary, see nostalgia and melancholia as essentially Victorian, as we also see as belonging to that era Thackeray's naive expectation that his closest friend, William Brookfield, should tolerate and comprehend his need of an *amitié amoureuse* with the latter's wife.

Obviously, the bulk of Thackeray's journalism was written for his contemporaries. The modern reader can afford to pass over substantially all of his nonfiction, and most of his short stories and novelettes, which accounts for half of the total oeuvre. There are many fine bits to be lost here, but, on the whole, the editorials and travel sketches are dated, the humorous skits a bit heavy, the short fiction obvious, and the burlesques obscure. It is not the author's fault that such transient prose has been bound in imposing volumes too grand for their content. Slightest of all is the art criticism. Thackeray had only the dimmest conception of the potentialities of painting. Anyone who doubts this should read him on Turner after reading Meyer Schapiro on Cézanne.

We are left, then, with the six major novels, *Vanity Fair, Pendennis, Esmond, The Newcomes, The Virginians,* and *The Adventures of Philip.* I shall now eliminate the last two. Thackeray had to struggle to make himself write novels at all, and in the end the struggle became too apparent. *The Virginians* is a pale sequel to *Esmond,* as *Philip* is to *Pendennis* and *The Newcomes.* What was Thackeray's reason for using the hero of *Pendennis* as the central observer in *The Newcomes* and *Philip?* As a device it is totally unsuccessful, for Thackeray has to reappear as the omniscient author whenever something happens that Pendennis could not naturally learn. What Thackeray is really doing is using Pendennis as a buffer between himself and the laborious job of telling his story. For the same reason, he saturates his chapters with his own reflections on the characters, on modern life, and on the plight of novelists. The curious thing about these "asides" is that they are *all* banal, *all* sentimental. They end by substantially destroying the reader's pleasure in the last two novels.

Of the four works left three have grave defects. *Pendennis* is flawed by a rambling plot, tedious dissertations on the London literary life, and a prig of a hero, but it is saved by the comic presentation of that outrageous old snob and diner-out, the major. *Esmond* is a gripping and vivid historical tale up to the death of Lord Castlewood, when it bogs down in heavy descriptions of contemporary literary and military events. *The Newcomes* is built around a great character, the colonel, but, like *Pendennis,* it contains wearisome sections about the hero's travels and efforts (totally unconvincing) to become a painter.

And so it seems that I have culled from a set of twenty-four volumes one perfect novel. *Vanity Fair* was the first of the six to appear, and there is hardly a hint in all the mass of Thackeray's pieces that preceded it to suggest that, at the age of thirty-seven, he would suddenly produce one of the great works of art of the century. The phenomenon deserves some attention.

When Thackeray died Thomas Carlyle observed of him: "He had many fine qualities, no guile or malice against any mortal; a big mass of soul, but not strong in proportion; a beautiful vein of genius lay struggling about in him." I think that this is the best expression of the problem that Thackeray's critics face. Where and what was the genius? Certainly, it is present throughout *Vanity Fair.* But why so particularly in that book and at that time? I suggest that Thackeray's own long struggle with poverty, and his bitter discovery of the roadblocks in the path of the genteel but unendowed, a struggle and a discovery that this very novel resolved and illustrated, had been waiting for the right fictional setting, and that this setting "found itself" (as Thackeray would have put it, in one of his favorite literal translations of French expressions) in the plight of two penniless women in a gilded, heartless world. Money, as one can read in Thackeray's immense correspondence, was the preoccupation of an anxious lifetime and the principal source of his creative impulse. Never again was he to find quite so fitting a *donnée*.

Money and women: that was the combination. It is a pity that he did not see this as clearly as that most self-conscious of all literary artists, Henry James, would have. If he had, he might not have devoted so much space in his later books to the financial problems of men. Carlyle said that Thackeray's social morality boiled down to the simple precept that a man should not be a snob, but he might have added another: that a man should not marry for money. Yet it is hard to imagine what else Thackeray's poor heroes could do to support themselves. Pendennis can make a pittance from his writing, but not enough; to live like a gentleman he needs his inheritance. Clive Newcome earns almost nothing from his painting; he has to be rescued by his cousin Ethel's invention of a legacy. And Philip Firmin, after failing both as a journalist and barrister, is bailed out only by a long lost will of a long deceased uncle turning up in a carriage pocket. Where could the genteel Victorian bachelor, who had no such deus ex machina in his prospects, find an income but at the altar?

If the reader be inclined to impatience with Thackeray's indolent and impractical young men and to surprise at his violent denunciation of the most obvious solution to their problems, he has still nothing but sympathy for the plight of the two women in *Vanity Fair*. Here Thackeray was dealing with a grave social problem, far too grave, as even he seemed to sense, to be solved by the trick of an invented or discovered inheritance. Becky Sharp and Amelia Sedley are faced with poverty. There is no way that either can go to work for her money without a dangerous loss of social status. Amelia, after a futile effort to sell her watercolors, has no alternative but to surrender her child to its grandfather in return for an income, and Becky must rely on her charm and wit, supported by a complete lack of scruple, to escape the degrading role of governess.

What is most honest in Thackeray here is that he controverts his own favorite precept by demonstrating that it is precisely an impecunious marriage that proves Becky's ultimate ruin. Her precipitate acceptance of Rawdon Crawley not only prevents her union with his rich father, who later proposes to her, but it costs Rawdon the legacy from a rich aunt which has been his only hope of independence. The marriage is doubly unlucky, for Rawdon has not only an empty purse but a full conscience, and he will ultimately destroy his wife's reputation by refusing to be a *mari complaisant*. Poor Becky! It is the only mistake that she makes in a career of magnificently calculated intrigue, but it is nonetheless a fatal one. Lord Steyne points the moral of the tale when he concludes, after watching with fascination the twisting and turning of this agile and brilliant creature, that she hasn't a chance, that without money she can never hope to make more than a brief splash in the torrent of the great world.

The financial plights of Becky and Amelia and their opposite but equally desperate ways of trying to cope with it, give to the novel a unity and a depth lacking in Thackeray's other fiction. I do not agree with the many commentators who have found Amelia insipid, and I suspect that a part of their difficulty stems from a suspicion that Thackeray meant them to admire her. But he didn't. He describes Amelia quite openly in his corespondence as a "silly little girl," and he professes to consider Dobbin an ass to be so taken in. But men *are* such asses. Thackeray had been one himself, and he knew it. Amelia is sufficiently pathetic in her dumb misery. She is financially ruined by an improvident husband; she can be rescued only by a man whom she stubbornly refuses to love. She pays the Victorian penalty of her sex: a man brings her low, and only a man can raise her.

Becky fights back. Gordon Ray points out that Thackeray makes her worse than she had to be, because only a thoroughly depraved woman, in the eyes of Victorians, could carry on so with Lord Steyne. Thus Becky must be shown as being brutal to her son, and, in the end, as the possible murderer of Joseph Sedley. I agree that she would be more plausible if she were allowed a few natural affections, but I think one sees so clearly the real character behind the Victorian screen that one can almost endow her with them. I find it difficult, for example, to take seriously the poor duped landlord of Becky's London house who ends in a debtors' prison, and I don't care *what* happens to Joseph Sedley. I am passionately on Becky's side all through the novel, yearning for her to get the best of a bloated, purse proud, hypocritical, boring society, and when she falls, like Lucifer, I feel that I am watching no less than a tragedy. What a world it is that clasps hands over her ruin: the prig, Pitt, the dissolute gambler, Rawdon, the smug Amelia, the imbecilic Dobbin! What had Becky given them all but a bit of life?

The arrest of Rawdon Crawley for debt immediately after Becky's presentation to the Prince Regent is the proof of what Steyne has said. For neither beauty, nor wit, nor sagacity, nor ingenuity, nor things amusing, nor things spiritual, will avail her anything if she has not wealth.

After *Vanity Fair* Thackeray's genius showed only fitfully, like the glimpses of the moon. It was clouded by sentimentality, by sermonizing, by tedious descriptions. The real trouble was that his urge to create was so much weaker than his urge to comment. He said that he envied Dickens the energy that exploded in such multiple characters and varied plots. Thackeray seemed now always to be doing the same thing and always to be taken in by his principal prototypes: the angry hero who, after basically swallowing the whole establishment, tries to preserve his individuality by bad manners, and the demure heroine, a slave to her husband, who attempts to seem free by making him listen to her prosy sermons. Thackeray could escape from mid-Victorian London only by taking refuge in the past, and in retreating there he took his own era with him, for if Henry Esmond and his two Warrington grandsons are not Victorians, then nobody ever was.

But like emerald islands in the Pacific that suddenly seem to spring out of a gray sea to the airborne observer, so do those portions of the later novels that are the fruit of Thackeray's genius emerge from his loquacity. I see Major Pendennis opening his invitations from earls and dukes at breakfast at his club while an envious acquaintance watches covertly from the next table; I see the major, expert diplomat that he is, upsetting his nephew's engagement to an actress and outwitting his own rebellious and blackmailing valet. And of course I see Colonel Newcome in all kinds of scenes, singing for his son's friends at a café in his strange falsetto, showing a childish little pride with his new wealth and a beautiful acceptance of bankruptcy, suffering patiently the beratings of his son's shrewish mother-in-law, threatening the wicked Barnes Newcome with a thrashing and finally dying in serene peace in a veterans' hospital. I see old, dyed, be-wigged Lady Castlewood defying the soldiers of King William who invade her bedchamber, and Lord and Lady Castle-wood tragically misunderstanding each other, and Beatrix dazzling the pretender, and Beatrix, ancient, as Baroness Bernstein . . . but I need not go on. When Thackeray was in the vein to write a dramatic scene, no one in his century could write a better.

Perhaps he was more skillful with characters who were wicked or ridiculous than those who were good. Except for Colonel Newcome his angels pay a heavy price for their halos. Who would not prefer to read about Lady Kew than Laura Pendennis? Or Barnes Newcome than Philip Firmin? Thackeray saw the vices of his time with a cold, clear eye. It is a pity that he was so impressed by its virtues. Nothing offers greater proof of the titanic complacency of the mid-Victorians than that they considered him a cynic!

I believe that *Vanity Fair* will be read as long as any nine-teenth-century British fiction is read. And it seems to me that readers who like *Vanity Fair* — at least some of them — may go on to *Esmond,* and *The Newcomes.* This may be a small percentage of a vast oeuvre, but it is still a substantial amount of fiction. In the struggle for survival Thackeray has been his own worst enemy.